Connect
5

Finding the Caring Adults *You may Not Realize* Your Teen Needs

KATHLEEN KIMBALL-BAKER
Foreword by Patty Wetterling

Search INSTITUTE

*Practical research
benefiting children
and youth*

**Connect 5: Finding the Caring Adults
You May Not Realize Your Teen Needs**
Kathleen Kimball-Baker

Copyright © 2004 by Search Institute

The contents of this book have been reviewed by a number of parenting and other professionals. Every effort has been made to provide sound advice; however, the information contained is not intended to take the place of appropriate counsel or other professional help in serious situations. The publisher and its reviewers take no responsibility for the use of any of the materials or methods described in this book, nor for the products thereof.

At the time of publication, all facts and figures cited herein are the most current available; all telephone numbers, addresses, and Web site URLs are accurate and active; all publications, organizations, Web sites, and other resources exist as described in this book; and all efforts have been made to verify them. The author and Search Institute make no warranty or guarantee concerning the information and materials given out by organizations or content found at Web sites that are cited herein, and we are not responsible for any changes that occur after this book's publication. If you find an error or believe that a resource listed herein is not as described, please contact Client Services at Search Institute.

Library of Congress Cataloging-in-Publication Data
Kimball-Baker, Kathleen, 1955–
    Connect 5 : finding the caring adults you may not realize your teen needs / Kathleen Kimball-Baker.
        p.   cm.
    Includes bibliographical references.
    ISBN 1-57482-848-7 (pbk. : alk. paper)
    1. Teenagers and adults. 2. Parenting. 3. Parent and teenager.
4. Interpersonal relations in adolescence. I. Title: Connect five. II. Title.
HQ799.2.A35K56 2004
649'.1—dc22   2004007040

10 9 8 7 6 5 4 3 2 1
Printed on acid-free paper in the United States of America.

Search Institute
615 First Avenue NE, Suite 125
Minneapolis, MN 55413
www.search-institute.org
612-376-8955 • 800-888-7828

Credits
Editor: Ruth Taswell
Design: Percolator
Production: Mary Ellen Buscher

For Sean, Laura, and Erik—my inspirations.

In memory of Laura Lee Geraghty (1945-2004),
who was good to so many young people.

Contents

I. Adults Who Know Your Teen

II. Other Caring Adults

III. Adults Who Provide
Specialized Services

IV. Activities to Try

Foreword

It is troubling how many people—even parents—are afraid of teens and turn away from them just at the time that they need to be most connected. Amid the often cultural and technological disconnects in today's world of the Internet and information overload, *Connect 5* shows adults how to provide teens with hope for a better world and with the means to better themselves safely. Thanks to author Kathleen Kimball-Baker, we are not only encouraged about what we can do, but also are shown the difference in other teens' lives that connections with caring, responsible adults have made.

In my first teaching experience, on a ship based near southern Maryland instructing math to high school dropouts to pass their GED (graduate equivalency degree), each student was asked upon entering the program: Is there one person you've connected with that's made a difference in your life? a parent who's encouraged you and believed in you? a teacher, a neighbor, a friend's older brother? If the reply was "No one," we teachers knew we had a long road ahead of us. The greatest barrier to these kids' success was to build their self-esteem enough to believe that they could succeed.

Many of my adult mentors when I was a child came through my parents having friends over at the house and knowing neighbors who would indeed report back to my parents any misdeeds of the five of us kids. I instilled the desire for such relationships in my own children and remember specifically one time that my daughter called my friend Judi. Carmen told Judi that I had gone to the store and would be right back but that she didn't want to be alone just then—would Judi talk to her until I returned. There are many times when we can't be there for our children. They need to be able to find adults who can help them and value them as the unique and special individuals that they are.

When you think about it, one of the wonderful things about being a teen is the opportunity to meet new friends and expand your world. Over the years, since my son's kidnapping on October 22, 1989, I have learned about the sexual exploitation of children and the fear of abduction. The many other cases before and after Jacob have caused a troubling side effect of a general mistrust of any and everybody in the communities where a child has been victimized. Parents still tell their children "Don't talk to strangers," even though we know the victimization most often comes from someone the family or the child knows.

I profess that it is far better, as parents, to teach kids and especially teenagers *how* to talk to people so that they learn boundaries as well as what is, and is not appropriate. This is especially true on-line where there are few boundaries and kids will often say things that they would never say to anyone in person.

Today's world is filled with many hardships that we, even the most sophisticated of us, don't understand. Our children are exposed to different challenges than we were as teens, they know different things than we do, and they solve problems differently than we would. It is too easy for us to be disconnected from their lives.

But kids want to be loved. They want and need to know their specialness. In fact, research shows that the number-one lure that works on teens in abduction situations is that of attention/affection. The strongest message kids will learn when they connect to others is that there are far more good people in the world than bad, and that there are many responsible, supportive people who can help and be with us through difficult and wonderful times.

Stay connected to your teens and enjoy in this book the many ways we can help our children benefit and connect with at least five more fabulous adults in their lives. I believe it will enrich children's lives and with that, everybody wins. Five. It can't be that hard.

Patty Wetterling
Co-founder
Jacob Wetterling Foundation
www.jwf.org

Acknowledgments

If someone asked me if I could name five people who support me, I'd have to say no. It's more like 500. Among those supporters is a cadre who made this book possible. I'd like to acknowledge them here.

Hats off to Ruth Taswell, a friend for many years and the very talented editor of this book. If you find it readable and glean some ideas to use, you can thank Ruth. She took on a very rough manuscript and a very busy author and made good things happen in a very big hurry!

Yet again, the publishing staff of Search Institute covered for me while I worked "offsite" (code for spending hours of writing time at the coffee shop). Thank you to Kay Hong for building such a strong, resilient team (and for being a friend to Laura); to Mary Ellen Buscher, for her unflappable approach to design direction, print production, and an absentee supervisor; to Tenessa Gemelke for story sleuthing, fact finding, and awesome editorial assistance; to Becky Aldridge for believing in this book and always pressing ahead; and to Julianne Schauer for the more than 300 chemical mood elevators known as chocolate!

Other Search Institute folks to whom I owe a debt of gratitude are Terri Swanson, who steamrolled (nicely, I might add) for book #2 while I was still learning to talk about book #1; Carol Paschke, Bill Kauffman, and JoAnn Holzemer—book promoters extraordinaire; Nancy Tellet-Royce for digging for great stories; members of the Product

Developers Team (some still here, others who've moved on) who scrutinized the proposal—Kalisha Davis, Gene Roelke-partain, Lynette Ward, Arturo Sesma, Rick Trierweiler, Anthony Strangis, and Cara Miller; to Peter Benson and Kent Eklund for the green light; and to Paul Kirst who liked the "numbers."

Special thanks to the fine reviewers of this manuscript: Ruth Taswell, Becky Aldridge, Tenessa Gemelke, Patricia Howell-Blackmore, Cara Miller, Terri Swanson, Mary Ackerman, Steven Bouffard, Sandra Harris, Connie Orrostieta, Taryn Gemelke, Nancy Stuckie, Gary Shannon, Kira Moscowitz, and Calvin Young.

From these people I have learned much about the power of adults who truly know how to connect with people (young and not-so-young)—Renie Howard, Beki Saito, Pam Weiner, Randy Baker, Nancy Lee, and Terri Sullivan. I thank you.

And as mine did, may your teens have the good fortune to connect with such good and caring people as Kay Kimball, Adele Della Torre, Spencer Kubo, Nakitto Lubega, Rochelle Taube, Wendy Holtzapple, Lynn Kiely, Loren Deutz, Wendy Holtzapple, David Lawson, Cecilia Erickson, Peter Erickson, Marge Ryan, Mark Ryan, Patricia Malloy, Patrick Curran, Denise DeVictoria, Ralph Greiling, Linda Greiling, Jacqueline White, Pam Hoopes, and Dan Kelliher. They put a face on asset 3!

A Story of Hope

My 15-year-old daughter and I are sitting at the dining-room table. It's been a tough talk, the kind that leaves you drained—of tears, of words, of imagination.

I have learned some things in the past hour that no parent ever wants to hear, things that make me question how a caring, adoring parent could have missed the signs of trouble or not figured out a way to intervene. I feel rotten. Worse, she feels bereft. We sit in exhausted silence for several minutes.

And then it hits me. The list. I need to show her the list.

I pull it down from the fridge, and she asks me what I'm doing. I tell her I want to show her something. (In a way, it's a teachable moment. But it's also a chance to move past the discomfort, to shift the attention away from what's gone wrong.) I explain that the list on this paper has a long, academic-sounding name—the developmental assets—but the list is filled with common sense: 40 things all kids need to succeed.

I ask her to look the list over and make a checkmark by those things she feels she has in her life. I know this is not the proper scientific method, but at that moment, I don't care. She checks off a bunch, and I tell her the good news: teens with that many assets are very likely to succeed.

And there it is, the first little sign. I feel as if I've been holding my breath for a year now, but, mercifully, there it is. She looks up at me, and in her tear-washed eyes, I see it. *Hope.*

The list has given her hope.

It's a tiny ember, and it needs some kindling. So, I take a chance. I ask her to look at what she did *not* check and pick something she'd like to have in her life. She mulls, and then quietly and ever-so-decisively she points to one. Her choice surprises me (but this time it's a good surprise). In hindsight, it was an especially wise choice this 15-year-old girl had made, one with a power that to this day amazes me—one that ultimately inspired this book.

She had picked Asset 3: Other Adult Relationships. The definition reads: *Young person receives support from three or more nonparent adults.*

There she was asking for more caring adults in her life. Not greater freedom, not a chance to hang out at the mall with friends, not more money, not permission to go to a rock concert. What she wanted was relationships with more adults. People who could see good things in her, people who wouldn't compete with her, categorize her, or judge her. People who could like her "as is."

What a simple concept. And the more I thought about it, the more I realized it wouldn't be hard to help make it happen.

Within days, I asked a handful of remarkable women I knew if they would spend a little time with my daughter. No one turned me down saying she was too busy or couldn't imagine being able to help. These women had met my daughter or heard my stories, and each saw in this 15-year-old girl qualities she truly liked or qualities that reminded her in some way of herself.

I had picked these women carefully, of course, trusting my hunch that they would make good adult friends. And they did. They reached out to my daughter immediately in their own unique ways—going for coffee, inviting her to a writing "retreat," singing together, listening, including her in important meetings. Through the friendships that unfolded with these women, my daughter strengthened her voice (artistically and personally) and her health. She learned that life goes on even after bad things happen, she felt respected, and she had fun—the kind of fun that doesn't cause a parent to worry.

But here's the part I didn't anticipate. These women did something wonderful for me—they let me be a parent.

Parenting is a tremendous responsibility—and at times it feels overwhelming. My husband and I have three children, each with her or his own needs over the years for clean clothes, meals, rides, homework help, college and career guidance, permission slips, privacy, affection, advice, space, school conferences, limits, friends, arts, sports. My daughter's adult friends, perhaps without even knowing it, helped me realize that as a parent, I truly did not and do not have to go it alone. I don't have to be all things at all times, and my kids are better off having more responsible caring adults in their lives. And very likely, I am a better parent for it, as well.

What's more—my daughter's adult friends felt genuinely enriched by knowing my daughter and had fun, too! Says Kay Hong, one of the adult friends:

> *I was honored to be asked. I could relate to Laura's struggles since I'd had a bit of trouble as a teen myself.*

We did some casual outings together and had interesting conversations in the car. I tried to listen more than lecture and was able to validate for her that her struggles were real and that she could come through them. I always get a warm greeting and hug from Laura when she's back in town from college. She knows that I am proud of her successes and care for her.

BACKED BY RESEARCH

My story has unique elements, but the basics are not unusual. A 2002 national poll of 1,005 American adults conducted by the YMCA of the USA and Search Institute (the nonprofit organization I work for) found that most parents surveyed feel they are "going it alone." No doubt, if you're the parent of a teen, you have had at least a few worrisome moments, maybe even a dining-room talk like the one my daughter and I had. It was my good fortune to know about the list of developmental assets and the power they have to help young people succeed.

Search Institute, whose mission is to provide leadership, knowledge, and resources to promote healthy children, youth, and communities, identified this list in the 1990s by examining research in the fields of prevention, psychology, and youth development. Over time, our researchers and many others have accumulated compelling evidence that it is in large measure through relationships with caring adults (parents and nonparents) that young people build many of the skills, strengths, and resilience—the developmental assets—they need to grow up happy and productive.

I can tell you that I have seen this in action—in the lives of my own children and in the lives of other kids.

THE NEED FOR MORE ASSET BUILDING

At Search Institute, when we use the word *assets*, we aren't talking money or property. We're talking *human* capital, the kinds of things that make people strong, resourceful, and happy. Think of developmental assets as "nutrients" for healthy growth. (Check out the lists of 40 developmental assets on pages 131–142.) Our surveys of hundreds of thousands of young people (in grades 6–12) in North America have shown that the more assets they report experiencing (e.g., caring neighbors, healthy boundaries, planning and decision-making skills, or personal qualities such as honesty and integrity), the fewer risky activities they engage in—and the more good choices they make.

Unfortunately, most young people don't have enough of these assets. The average number of assets they report is about 19. Fewer than half report experiencing the asset that my daughter said she wanted in her life—Other Adult Relationships. While adults we've surveyed tell us they believe strongly that they should play a role in ensuring the healthy development of young people, they just don't make the effort to get to know other people's kids (your kids) in a way that would help to build the developmental assets kids need to succeed.

WHY THE DISCONNECT?

Many barriers keep adults and teens from connecting in meaningful ways—television, computer games, and headphones, for starters. But a big part of the problem is that, by and large, we as parents don't *invite* caring adults into the lives of our teens often enough.

Most of us feel as if we're doing a pretty good job of being parents, and when times get tough, we try to carry on as best we can. Some of us feel as if it's not okay to admit to needing help or it doesn't even occur to us to ask—our own friends, coworkers, relatives, neighbors, empty nesters, and parents of our teens' friends. Or we're so busy just trying to get through the day, asking for help feels like another "to do" item. Even when we do ask, some of us worry we'll encounter the rejection of "No, sorry, can't."

But here's the surprising truth: many adults Search Institute has surveyed and talked to over the years believe they *should* be supporting young people and want to find ways to do so, but they're worried about offending *you* as a parent, having *their* offers be rejected, or simply not having what it takes to be a friend to a young person.

So, what happens when we as parents don't ask for help from other adults, and other adults don't offer?

Simple: our kids lose out. And so do we as parents.

Sadly, this unfortunate disconnection has become a generally accepted way of behaving in our society. For most young people today, it's standard to *not* have plenty of caring, involved adults in their lives. Yet solid evidence indicates that having more of these adults in young people's lives is a predictor of their well-being and success.

Clearly, the standard needs to change. In this book, I suggest some steps to try. I was fortunate to find caring adult friends for my daughter, and so can you. History shows that when individual people, like you and me, take action, we can change pervasive ways of thinking and being. Past standards such as "a woman's place is in the kitchen" are no longer acceptable because individual people saw the harm they were causing to society. Similarly, as parents, we can change the standard for our kids, ourselves, and our society by inviting caring, responsible adults into the lives of our teens.

GIVING KIDS WHAT THEY NEED—AND WANT

Young people need and *want* adult friends, even when it seems they're giving us signals that they want more independence. Does that surprise you? It certainly did me.

But years of research confirm that young people truly value relationships with adults—their own parents, for example, and teachers, coaches, informal mentors, and others who support them. In my own encounters, conversations, and interviews with young people over the years, I've been struck by how poignant their longing for connection to good adults really is. Many wonder why adults either scowl at them suspiciously or, worse, look right past them as if they don't exist. They've told me they yearn for warm, trusting relationships with responsible adults who listen, help them think through decisions, look beyond their appearance, and see their good qualities.

Isn't it ironic, then, that just when teens want adults to help them do the important work of growing up, they feel the most disconnected?

As parents, we are in an excellent position to connect our teens with the kinds of adults who can teach them new skills and help them take the long view, listen without judgment and lighten the mood—and support the values we work so hard to instill. We still know our teens best, even as they go through the rapid developmental changes and the emotional ups and downs of adolescence. We can help find the kinds of adults who'll make good friends.

HOW THIS BOOK CAN HELP

The numerous ideas, tips, and inspiring stories you'll find in this book will help to get you thinking about ways to connect other trustworthy adults with your teen and other teens you know. The ideas in here are for all teens, wherever they are, whatever their background is, whether they're struggling through troubling issues or not, have special needs, identify with a minority group, succeed in school, a sport, or another activity, or simply don't think they need adult attention. No young person can ever have too many supportive adults in his or her life. Keep in mind, too, that there's no need to wait until a child is a teen. The earlier parents start connecting other responsible adults with their kids, the better. The ideas I suggest cover:

- Engaging more fully the *adults who already know your teen*—relatives, parents of friends, employers, coaches;

- Identifying *other caring adults* you could invite into your teen's life—your own friends, coworkers, a retiree;

- Capitalizing on times when your teen might connect with *adults who provide specialized services*—tutors, therapists, and physicians; and

- Locating *activities to try,* join, or organize that will put your teen in contact with groups of adults— after-school programs, volunteer work, congregations, special events—where relationships can begin.

Pick a few of the ideas to start with. Not all may work just right for you and your teen's circumstances. Sometimes, involving an adult friend in your teen's life is about creating an opportunity or taking advantage of a situation for a relationship to happen. It may simply be about how you encourage your teen to relate to a certain adult. Some connections may develop over time or have a huge impact with just one interaction. Not every relationship your teen has with an adult friend needs to result in a long-lasting, deep bond to be meaningful and significant.

Acting on the ideas can help to change the standard so that far more caring, responsible adults are involved in the lives of our teens. Today, nearly 600 communities across North America (and now in Australia and South Africa, too) identify themselves as Healthy Communities • Healthy Youth (HC • HY) initiatives, a national effort Search Institute launched seven years ago to support individuals, organizations, communities, even entire states, to build developmental assets with young people. Their work shows that everyone can be an *asset builder*—someone who intentionally does good things with and for youth, and in doing so, is helping to strengthen the community and our young people.

WHY 5?

I chose the number 5 not so much to say that's the minimum or maximum number of caring adults our kids need, but because it's a good target number to aim for.

Derek Petersen, co-founder of Alaska's statewide initiative, an amazing asset builder, and a powerful spokesperson for building intergenerational relationships, speaks eloquently about this concept. When he talks about the importance of connecting young people and adults, he suggests that parents ask their kids to "name five caring people" in their lives. You hope, says Petersen, that you're one of those people, but you can count your blessings if there are mostly adults among those five names. That's a good sign, he continues, that your child is getting the support—and very likely the developmental assets—he or she needs to grow up happy, confident, and capable.

Think of the adults your child names as your partners—thank them and let them know how important they are to you and your teen. Be on the lookout for more caring, trustworthy adults to connect your son or daughter with—no teen can have too many! And if you don't hear five adults named, this book will help you to change that.

KEEP YOUR EYES OPEN

There is, unfortunately, the possibility that your child at some point will meet with an uncaring adult, or even one who will try to cause your child harm. It's one of the biggest worries we have as parents when we let our kids out of our sight.

Not *all* the adults who want to be with kids want to do them good; some may want to take advantage of them. There are adults who are expert liars and manipulators, who target children and adolescents as victims, who dupe parents into trusting them, and who get away with hurting kids over and over. You only have to watch the evening news or read the daily newspaper to learn of instances of coaches, priests, teachers, neighbors, and parents who have hurt kids.

But the tremendous benefits—and importance—of connecting kids with adults are far too great to be dismissed by frightening realities. We as individuals and as a society can and must protect our children in a *balanced* way—one that lowers their risk of becoming victims and *also* makes sure they're connected to the responsible adults who are such an important part of their healthy growth and development. We know this is possible. The encouraging stories in this book provide strong evidence from people in many different kinds of communities who have taken their role as asset builders to heart.

Most of us already try to teach our kids to keep away from dangerous people, to stay safe, to know that they have a right to the privacy of their bodies, and to turn to us when they're worried, confused, or feel "creepy" about someone.

So what more can we do to be careful when we seek to connect our kids with other adults?

TAKE OFF THE BLINDERS

Our first line of protection, according to world-renowned psychologist Anna C. Salter, Ph.D., an expert on people who prey on other people (children and adults), is to take our blinders off and be a little skeptical all the time. In her book about predators,* she cautions that it is our misconceptions about predators that make us vulnerable to them. Usually, they're not the "monsters" most expect them to be, but charming, likable people who use those traits to hide their real intentions and carefully plan their activities. "Assume that every coach, every priest, every teacher is not *likely*" to be a predator but that "one *could* be and that you will not know if he is," suggests Salter. (The "he" is intentional here; the vast majority of predators are in fact men, although there are some female predators.)

The crimes committed by offenders are scary things to name and talk about—molestation, sexual abuse, rape, kidnapping—but important ones to address, Salter urges. As is recognizing that every profession that involves children and youth will attract a few people who prey on children.

KNOW WHAT'S GOING ON

As parents, we must be wary and selective, and monitor our kids' activities and who coaches or counsels them. But since there's no checklist for detecting child molesters and rapists consistently, according to Salter, we must pay attention to a few simple, specific strategies:

---

*Salter, Anna C. 2003. *Predators: Pedophiles, Rapists, and Other Sex Offenders: Who They Are, How They Operate, and How We Can Protect Ourselves and Our Children.* New York: Basic Books.

- *Be present:* Show up at school, at practices, at rehearsals. Regularly attending your teen's extracurricular activities helps her or him appear less vulnerable.

- *Be particularly wary of certain men* who have no family of their own, do not appear to date adults of either gender, and spend time only with kids, especially if they have no kids of a similar age of their own.

- *Double your suspicions* if someone in a high-risk group (see characteristics above) seeks out your teen, gives her or him small gifts, or tries to see her or him outside the boundaries of the activity.

- *Keep in mind* that predators have perfected the ability to hide the cues that usually make people spot untruthfulness. They typically don't avert eye contact or fidget. They work hard to build up trust with parents of the child they target, and may prey on especially vulnerable kids. Even if these predators feel horrible about what they're doing, they don't show it.

- *Monitor* your teen's use of the Internet.

By all means, if you have any suspicions, trust your instincts. And if your teen has the courage to report a problem to you, believe him or her, even if what you're hearing seems unimaginable. Too many bad people get away with hurting kids because people—including parents—dismiss or get angry about what kids report, assume they're lying, exaggerating, or trying to get attention, or can't even imagine that what the child is reporting is possible because it runs so contrary to the predator's public image.

STAY CONNECTED

Worries about predators, taken to an extreme, can tempt us to keep our kids away from other adults, but it's important that we protect our kids in a *balanced* way. We need to keep our eyes open all the time *and* connect our kids with the good adults, the caring, responsible people who are an essential part of their healthy development.

It's also important to remember that even young people who have been victims can find the presence of trustworthy adults in their lives part of the process of healing. If I didn't believe that the benefits outweigh the risks, I would never have written this book. In the best of all worlds, we could keep all children safe all the time. In this less-than-perfect one, we can at least keep them connected to good adults.

STILL WONDERING?

Perhaps you're thinking, "Even if I should—and want—to connect my teen with a caring adult, he (or she) is too shy . . . doesn't warm to my ideas . . . or seems too grouchy to be likable to anyone else." Nagging thoughts can waylay good intentions, but you really are the one who is in the best position to connect your teen with trustworthy adults. To help you set aside some other common concerns besides safety, I've included a section at the end of the book called "Frequently Stated Worries" (see pages 120–127) that offers some specific suggestions and extra encouragement.

Perhaps, though, you're just perplexed about how to get started or how to actually ask caring adults to be a part of your teen's life. It is a risk to extend yourself beyond your comfort zone, but try not to let fears keep you from asking for what is an essential part of your teen's growth and development—caring relationships with many adults. As you're reading this book, consider the following:

- *Think back on your own teen years.* Can you remember someone who was especially supportive of you? Someone who refused to give up on you even when others were throwing their hands up in despair? Someone who stood up for you? Someone who took the time to get to know you? Someone who introduced you to fun hobbies or interesting ideas? Those are the kinds of adults your teen needs, too. As you scan the list of ideas in the table of contents, see if any point to a connection that you might not have considered before.

- *Take a careful look at the list of developmental assets* (pages 131–142) and note those you think your teen has. Do you see any that you'd like to focus on? Do those particular assets bring to mind any adults you know or *types* of adults you know that might be of help? Does your son need a tutor to improve in a class? Are there volunteer activities in which your daughter can demonstrate her leadership skills?

- *Ask your teen to look at the list of developmental assets.* When teens can identify and articulate what they feel as well as choose what they'd like, they're more likely to feel hopeful and empowered and connect with others.

- *Think about your teen's strengths.* Think about adults you know who have the same kinds of strengths (or qualities or traits) as your teen. See if there's a possible connection to be made. Their similarities provide an easy conversation starter.

  Remember, too, there's almost always a flip side to those qualities in your teen that you may not consider a strength. Your teen's sarcasm, for example, may also show up as keen wit.

- *Ask other adults in whatever way works best for you.* I'm an extrovert, so it's easy for me to ask. But I also understand that the fear of rejection can be paralyzing. Sometimes, just being straightforward is the simplest approach. For example, you could say, "My son has asked to have more caring adults in his life. You seem to always appreciate my stories about him. Would you like to get to know him more directly?" Or, you could try, "I'm finding that I don't always have as much time as I would like to spend with my daughter. She's really interested in historic architecture, and I know you are, too. Would you like to get to know her and share your interest?"

I've come to believe that the vast majority of people actually *like* to be asked questions—and truly *welcome* the opportunity to help. Keep in mind, too, how rewarding these friendships can be for *adults*. In one study** of teens and the adults who became "very important people" in their lives, more than 90 percent of the adults in those relationships said their number-one reason for being involved with the youth was that their young friend was "fun to be with."

The highly respected psychologist Urie Bronfenbrenner, Ph.D., professor emeritus of Human Development and Family Studies and of Psychology at Cornell University in Ithaca, New York, says that all children need someone in their lives who is "simply crazy about them." As parents, we're usually their number-one "crazy" adults. But imagine how lucky our children would be if we could add a few more to their lives.

So get ready to connect 5 and watch the good things that will unfold for your teen—and for you as a parent.

**Beam, M. R., Chen, C., & Greenberger, E. 2002. The nature of adolescents' relationships with their "very important" nonparental adults. *American Journal of Community Psychology*, 30(2), 305–325.

I

Adults Who Know Your Teen

If you think about all the adults who already know your teen and choose a few of them to get more involved in your teen's life, you'll soon see how easy it is to get started—and this group may even provide connections with more than five adults. In this section, you'll find various ways to more fully engage them in your teen's life.

Aunts and Uncles

It's not uncommon for a young person to find in an aunt or uncle a familiar quality, trait, or preference that doesn't exist in one parent or the other—like being extroverted, or enjoying playing basketball, or preferring bananas rather than jelly with peanut butter sandwiches.

When Terri Sullivan, a graduate student in Cambridge, Massachusetts, decided she would not have children of her own, she also realized she had a unique opportunity—she could take the time to build lasting bonds with each of her nephews, even the ones in faraway Ireland. Every summer, she visits them for two weeks. Terri believes in the power of developmental assets and has chosen to live out those beliefs in a very personal way.

If you have a sibling or sister- or brother-in-law who is a favorite with your teen, let him or her know. Then do what you can to encourage the two of them getting together. With all of the different family configurations we have these days, an adult stepsibling from a previous marriage may also be a good choice.

- *If you can't attend an event* at your teen's school, ask a special aunt or uncle to go in your place.

- *Encourage your teen* and her or his aunt or uncle to take a class or trip together, or suggest a regular time to get together.

- *If a favored aunt* has only sons, perhaps she'd like more contact with your daughter doing an activity they both enjoy; an uncle who has only girls might appreciate special time with a nephew.

- *If you have to be out of town,* maybe an aunt or uncle could help out and make it the start of an annual weekend event with your teen.

- *Check with your local YMCA or YWCA* or community center to see if it offers activities for teens and special relatives.

- *Encourage an aunt or uncle* to write letters, send e-mails, or telephone. They don't have to live nearby or appear in person to develop a supportive relationship with your teen.

Your teen's aunts or uncles may already be doing many of the things that help build assets, but intentional efforts can make even more of a difference. When young people can spend time with special aunts and uncles, the whole family benefits.

Grandparents

Stories abound of the powerful bonds children build with their grandparents.

When Elliott Royce of St Louis Park, Minnesota, became a grandfather for the first time, he asked his son, Jeff, what kind of gift he should give the baby boy. "The best gift you can give him isn't money and it isn't material," responded Jeff. "It's you and the time you spend with him."

Elliott took that wish to heart—a very big heart. Whenever he was in the neighborhood, he took both of his grandsons, David and his brother, Michael, on little "errands"—for example, a visit to a man who makes and sells Medieval-era swords. Over the years, he has introduced the boys to all kinds of interesting people, occupations, and activities. As teens now, David and Michael have delved into some adventuresome pastimes, no doubt encouraged by their grandfather— David at 19 is already a talented glass blower, and Michael, 16, an accomplished youth circus trapeze performer!

Tenessa Gemelke, an assistant editor at Search Institute, says her grandfather, who wasn't especially comfortable with teens, found the perfect way to keep a strong relationship with her during her middle and high school years. The two connected around a mutual interest—theater. Her grandfather would take her to every new production at the local dinner theater, and they talked about the costumes, sets, plots, and performances, even though they didn't always share the same opinions.

Many of today's grandparents live more active lives than did their own grandparents, but they also often live great distances from their children and grandchildren. Some travel agencies, such as Grandtravel or Senior Women's Travel, now even promote national and international tours designed especially for grandparents and grandchildren.

Some ways to encourage more interaction between teens and grandparents include:

- Your teen sitting down with a grandmother or grandfather to capture special family recipes or stories on paper, audiotape, or videotape or to hear stories about you as a child;

- Going through old photo albums together and making sure everyone is properly identified;

- Comparing the worst fashion trends each can remember seeing; and

- Talking about their heroes.

3

Parents of Your Teen's Friends

Some of the nicest friendships my teens have had are with a parent of one of their peers.

Many times such relationships simply happen on their own. Linda Davich of West St. Paul, Minnesota, who is a single mom, says that her 14-year-old son Matthew tends to be a good influence on his friends: "As a result, their parents are grateful and fond of him. He has grown closer to these adults, and now I think of them as extra sets of parents for my son."

Some connections your teen may make with others' parents may begin from a different perspective, say, through a coworker or by babysitting. Such relationships may begin with you making a point of meeting the parents of your teen's friends—go inside when you drop your teen off for a sleepover. Chat on the phone for a bit, introduce yourself at a school concert, game, or assembly, or get acquainted over coffee.

Younger teens might object about you talking to their friends' parents this way. Assure them it's all part of getting acquainted and creating a supportive network of caring adults for them. Later, they'll appreciate your paying attention, even if they roll their eyes at you now.

Some parents may not be sure how comfortable you are with them forming such friendships with your teen. They might feel they need permission from you to have conversations about their values, politics, opinions about money, or spiritual beliefs. But those kinds of conversations let teens explore ideas in a safe setting and express and test out their own thoughts.

Be sure to let the parents of your teen's friends know what your comfort level is. It's also a good idea to tell them what your expectations are for your teen's behavior at their home. Encourage them to be clear about boundaries and let you know if they see activities they don't think are appropriate.

4

Your Teen's Employer

In addition to providing spending money, part-time jobs can offer your teen an excellent opportunity to connect with responsible adults. How satisfying this experience is will largely depend on the bond he or she forms with the supervisor, shift manager, team leader, or an older coworker or employee.

For teens new to employment, building work-based relationships is uncharted territory—a little rough at times, confusing at others, and often anxiety-provoking. If young people can build a strong, honest relationship with their bosses from the start, it can help the experience go more smoothly.

Obviously, you can't build this relationship *for* your teen, but you certainly can help her or him learn how to do this on her or his own. Here are some tips:

- *Share stories of your first work experiences* and what you wish you had done differently or what went well.

- *Talk about the best supervisors* you've ever had and what you liked about them.

- *Let your teen know that good communication* with his or her supervisor is essential—calling when running late is appreciated, as is giving plenty of notice when time away from work is needed.

- *If you have a friend who has supervised teens* at some point in her or his career, invite the friend to join you and your son or daughter for dinner or hot chocolate or a walk. Ask a few questions about what behaviors build a strong relationship with the boss. Encourage your friend to share what pitfalls to avoid.

- *Some teens worry* about coming across as "brown-nosing" or trying to become a boss's favorite. Help your teen see that behaving *professionally,* with both coworkers *and* supervisors, is expected in any job—and, is the best way to earn better pay and opportunities.

Even if a first employment experience doesn't work out, encourage your teen to identify what he or she learned and would do differently.

My daughter's first real job was made possible by her hair stylist. She encouraged the owner of the salon to hire Laura, 14 at the time, to work part-time to answer phones and make appointments. Laura's performance didn't quite measure up to expectations, and she worked there only briefly. But Laura's work habits strengthened with each subsequent job, and she got wonderful reviews at her last summer job at a deli. And what's more, she still sees the stylist, who remains a caring adult in her life!

5

Coaches

A special coach can make all the difference in whether an individual player feels that he or she really matters, regardless of skill or how the team is doing.

Don Berry of Mason City, Iowa, is that kind of coach.* "We didn't have a great season," says Alex Bohl, a student in grade 8 on the little league team Don coached. (Their final record was 1-14-1.) "But Coach Berry made it a fun season. During the games, we'd usually be down by a lot, but he'd keep our hopes up. He'd tell us, 'There's always another game.'"

Don, a juvenile probation officer and three-time competitive triathlete, was nominated by Alex as a "hidden hero" in the community. He helped Alex, an excellent athlete, "learn to have patience with kids who didn't have the same skill level and to respect the fact that they were trying." Don was also known for calling individual players after the games to point out what they'd done well in the game.

---

*"Don Berry wins big with a losing season," *Assets Magazine,* Spring 2001, 14.

Part of engaging coaches in your teen's life more fully is letting them know how much you appreciate their efforts, even when the team isn't winning. Other ways to help your teen connect with a good coach include:

- *Encouraging your teen to show up for practices* on time, work hard, be polite, and listen for ways to improve skills. Understandably, coaches can feel annoyed with players who goof off or act disrespectfully, and that's not going to help the relationship.

- *Helping your teen view decisions* the coach makes from the coach's point of view. Your teen may occasionally feel excluded from playing. Part of forming good relationships is being able to see the other person's point of view.

- *Recommending that your teen approach* the coach respectfully and honestly if there's a conflict with the coach. Support your teen, but try not to resolve the conflict yourself. Keep encouraging your teen to take the "high road" and not to resort to sulking or outbursts. Coaches appreciate when players act maturely—and that's good for their ongoing connection.

Great coaches know players want to win, but they also know each one is learning how to build important assets— how to get along with others, resolve conflict, plan ahead, care about and help others, and increase self-esteem. Coaches in nonsports activities, such as speech, debate, or mock trial, can be valuable connections for your teen as well.

6

Music Teachers

"The teachers who have made a difference in my life have always been music teachers." So noted entertainer Shari Lewis, best known for her act with the endearing puppet character, Lamb Chop, in a book* about special teachers.

Piano teachers, voice coaches, band directors, and music teachers of all kinds are often memorable mentors for young people. When a young person and an adult can connect in a very special relationship around a shared interest and passion for music, it opens many opportunities for meaningful conversation and growth—about such things as:

- Expressing emotion creatively;

- Sticking to a task, even when it feels boring;

- Challenging oneself to reach a new skill level;

---

*Quoted in Bluestein, J. 1995. *Mentors, masters, and Mrs. MacGregor: Stories of teachers making a difference.* Deerfield, Florida: Health Communications, Inc., p.102.

- Avoiding behaviors that can hurt musical ability (abusing alcohol or smoking);

- Planning ahead (for auditions and competitions);

- Dealing with performance anxiety;

- History and famous musicians;

- Ethnic, cultural, and regional differences;

- What it takes to get into college to pursue music; or

- How to turn making music into a career.

How do you find a good music teacher who's also a good fit for your teen? Here are a few tips:

- *Word of mouth*—Have your teen ask his or her friends to recommend memorable music teachers. Ask other parents or middle or high school music teachers.

- *Know your teen's learning style*—Will stricter practicing demands help your son or daughter stay on task or set up a potential conflict between student and teacher? Is the teacher comfortable with a more casual approach? Try a lesson or two first before committing.

- *Agree on goals*—Is the teacher open to letting your teen learn to play the type of music he or she would prefer (e.g., jazz instead of, or along with, classical)?

II

Other Caring Adults

Many adults who have had unique experiences or are passionate about their work can also make a big impact in your teen's life. Even if you—or your teen—have not previously met them, a simple invitation can bring about a welcomed, safe, caring connection. While your child may not connect with every adult you introduce her or him to, by increasing the number of opportunities, you increase the chances of a trustworthy relationship developing.

7

Adults Your Teen Picks

Your son or daughter may have already identified a caring adult he or she would like to know better—but likely no one's asked, nor has your teen thought to mention it on his or her own.

So go ahead—ask. Show your son the list of assets and talk about how building developmental assets contributes to becoming a healthy, happy, successful man. Ask your daughter to identify the assets she'd like to build and who pops up in her mind as someone with whom she'd love to spend some time—or perhaps *more* time.

If your teen has identified people you know, there's no time like the present to get on the phone and chat a bit about how you're interested in connecting your teen to more caring adults and that you'd love their help. I know this works—I did it myself, and both my teen and the adults she got to know found their time together rewarding.

If your teen suggests someone you've got reservations about, ask some more questions and express your concerns and explain why. Perhaps your teen likes a skill or quality that this person has, and you can redirect your son or daughter to someone with that same skill or quality whom you feel more comfortable about. Or if it's someone you don't know, get to know that adult first, meet in person in a public place, and trust your instincts.

8

A Friend of Your Own

As parents, we're often relieved and genuinely thrilled to hear a friend say something positive about our child or be amused by her or his antics. But such comments are really telling us much more.

Your friend has a fresh perspective on your teen, one you might not be able to see while you're in the throes of a conflict. (I have several friends who did just this for me—and became friends with my teenage daughter.)

Here are a couple of clues that such a connection could happen:

- You've just vented to a friend about your teen and a frustration you're having, and your friend grins and says: "What a cool kid!"

- Your friend makes note of a quality she or he has in common with your teen or says something like "Wow, I was just like that when I was Jim's age" or "I can relate to how sensitive Ella is—I still feel like that at times!"

- Your teen lights up when your friend stops by for a visit or phones you.

- Your teen seems eager to hear what your friend's opinions are on the latest news or sports event, election, movie, or singer-songwriter.

Ask your friend if he or she would be willing to spend a little time with your teen—coming along to a recital or over for a game of cards, going to a movie or to a sports event. Chances are, your friend would love the opportunity but hasn't exactly figured out how to offer without making it sound as if he or she is intruding, questioning your ability to parent.

Let your friend know the invitation is open.

9

A Coworker

Consider inviting a coworker to your teen's game, play, recital, science fair, or art exhibit, especially if your coworker had or continues to have a special interest in that arena as well. Make sure the two have an opportunity to chat. You'll be surprised how much they have in common and how enriched they'll both be by the connection they're likely to form.

I dutifully invited my daughter Laura every April to Take Our Daughters And Sons to Work® Day from the time she was age 9 till age 14. The year she turned 15, it occurred to me that she expected the invitation, yet I knew it was likely to be a pretty ho-hum experience to come with me yet again.

So I asked a coworker if she would be willing to let my daughter "shadow" her that day.

Not only did my coworker, Beki, say yes, but she could hardly wait. She told me that she loved teens like Laura, those who have strong opinions, question authority, and possess a restless, creative side. I was surprised (pleasantly so, mind you) to hear that there were people who actually appreciated those qualities in teens, the same qualities that sometimes made it challenging to be a parent.

Beki took my daughter to a United Way meeting on how to spend money for youth and family programs. Laura ended up contributing her thoughts to the group, and the committee liked her ideas so much, they invited her to become a full-fledged member.

Later, Beki showed up at a play that Laura was directing in high school, toting flowers and brimming with genuine interest in Laura's work. My daughter has never forgotten that, and she counts Beki as one of her favorite adults.

10

An Empty Nester

A once-active household can go quiet pretty quickly when the last child turns 18 and moves on. Contrary to conventional wisdom, parents who've just emptied their "nests" may not be ready to "fly the coop" themselves just yet. Some might welcome the opportunity to stay busy by spending time with teens—yours, to be exact.

Think about it. They've had plenty of experience and likely made a few mistakes but now have some perspective and wisdom. What might seem like a crisis to you as a parent may very well seem like a "this, too, shall pass" moment to them. Wouldn't you welcome that kind of reassurance? Wouldn't your teen?

When I flipped out because my daughter bleached her hair blonde without asking for permission, she cried, "Mom, it's just hair! It'll grow." I probably would have taken it more calmly if I had known a parent who had previously been through the crazy period of a teen trying out new hairstyles. An empty nester could have reassured my daughter that I'd get over it, too, and maybe even shared a chuckle with her.

The baby boomer set is just bulging with empty nesters or *near*-empty nesters. How do you find them?

- Do you have a friend from high school or college who started a family before you?

- What about those parent volunteers at the high school whose last child at home is graduating?

- You could also look around your neighborhood, congregation, lodge, softball team, civic association, workplace, reading group, or bowling league.

11

A Local Political Candidate

Many candidates for local elections go door-to-door to talk about their ideas, get acquainted, and drum up support. When one comes knocking on your door, how about asking him or her to spend a few minutes talking to your teen, too?

Here are a few questions you and your teen could ask the candidate:

- What are you doing to support young people in the community?

- What stands have you taken in the past that show you really care about *teens*? (Many people talk about how they want the best for children, but their emphasis tends be for *younger* children. So be sure to press about the teen issue.)

- What do you do personally to build developmental assets? What will you do to build developmental assets in the community if you win the election?

- How will you focus on what's *right* about teens, rather than just trying to fix what people think is wrong?

- In what ways do you see teens as a resource to the community? How have you involved teens in your campaign?

Then talk with your teen about the answers the candidate gave. Ask if he or she thought the candidate worked to make a connection with him or her. If your teen liked the candidate, maybe he or she would enjoy volunteering on the campaign.

One of my teens did just that with a friend—they distributed literature for a candidate for Minneapolis park commissioner. They knew he had volunteered on youth sports activities and supported them in a big way.

Of course the political arena can often be confusing, especially for a young teen, let alone adults. Politicians are often really good at building support—that's what can make them so successful. Encourage your teen to keep her or his mind open. What's important in the process is that young people learn to weigh the pros and cons and use their heads as much as their hearts.

12

Librarians

More and more librarians are seeing the value of making libraries teen-friendly places. They believe it's important to foster a love of reading, but they also see that how they interact with young people can build a lifelong relationship with the library as well—and that's a good thing for a society built on the principle of informed citizens.

In Fort Bend County, Texas (an area just southwest of Houston), library staff has trainings during which they role-play what it's like to be a nervous teen coming in for last-minute help on a report. Then they compare how librarians treat adults in search of information. Their aim is to remind themselves how hard it is to ask for help when you're young and inexperienced, and how important it is for staff to be patient, understanding, interested, and attentive.

Molly Krukewitt, retired youth services librarian, tells an amazing story about a small group of younger teens who tended to loiter at the library in Richmond, Texas. When noise and disruption became too much of an issue, Molly's supervisor instructed her to go deal with the kids and make sure they didn't come back. Molly, who knew about developmental assets, decided to try a different tack. She walked over to the group, asked them to join her in a meeting room, and then posed the following question: How can the library improve its services for young people?

"At that point I knew I had their attention," she laughs. What these kids wanted was a "safe place to chill." So Molly offered to open a meeting room to them on Monday nights, show movies, and make popcorn. The youth were thrilled with the idea, and the group ballooned to 50 in less than one month. The youth have also used the time and place to hold poetry competitions and "talk-show" events.

You can be sure that librarians are encountering teens regularly and would find positive encounters with young people refreshing. Encourage your teen to:

- Work with a librarian to learn good study habits and how to use the library resources productively.

- Be respectful and quiet in quiet areas of the library, and show appreciation—maybe sending a thank-you card when a librarian has been especially helpful.

- Go to the library with you.

- Volunteer with you to organize shelves or help with a children's program.

- Attend a local Friends of the Library U.S.A. meeting to support libraries.

13

A Chaperone

Adults who volunteer to chaperone a group of young people to a sports tournament or on a band or field trip very likely enjoy the company of teens—and have a high tolerance for the noise and chaos that can accompany those events. I happen to be one of them, and I look forward to the special friendship that inevitably develops with one or two of the kids on the trip.

While accompanying a high school choir to Nashville last year, I connected with a young woman who I knew was going through a hard time in her life. Facing some similar difficulties myself, which I was able to share with her, we soon hit it off. I was so honored when she invited me to her graduation open house.

If your child is planning to go on a trip with a school or youth group, find out who'll be chaperoning. Feel free to ask for phone numbers of those adults who will be chaperoning and give them a call before the trip to get acquainted. Be careful not to reveal anything that will embarrass your teen, but certainly let the chaperones know helpful information.

Find out a little something about the chaperones, too, so that you can share it with your son or daughter, and they don't start off as strangers—the connection may be the beginning of something more long term.

You can let chaperones know in advance any worries you have for your kids. Perhaps it's their shyness, food allergies, or an injury or medical problem that might need looking after but that your teen doesn't want to call attention to. When I've chaperoned, I always appreciate getting these little bits of information—they've given me an opening to start talking and helped me get to know individual kids more quickly.

An Expert

Don't underestimate how honored an expert might feel to be asked to share his or her knowledge with young people. Especially if it's an uncommon field of work, the expert will likely be happy to have a young person show interest and may even be willing to take on an apprentice.

Has your son or daughter expressed an interest in a particular area? Car repair? Weaving? Geography? Forestry? Science fiction? Cooking? Philosophy? Running a small business? Fishing? Space travel? Alternative healing? A musical instrument not offered in school? Make a call to someone in that field and see if you can arrange a visit.

Sometimes, as parents, we hear ideas from our kids pop up, and we may dismiss them because we can't see exactly how our children could "fit" the mold or make a living in such a field. But even if these are passing interests for our kids, they are also opportunities to connect them to interesting, caring adults who know something about these areas.

My youngest son always enjoyed tagging along with me to garage sales. He would make a beeline for the tables with jewelry and pour over the offerings. One day, I had to visit a silversmith to repair a ring and, remembering Erik's interest in jewelry, I asked the craftsman if my son could watch him in action. The silversmith was delighted to be asked and showed Erik one of the steps in making a ring. Every time we pass that shop he remembers fondly that encounter and how kind the proprietor was to take the time to interact with him.

A Teacher Who Can Relate

If you're lucky and your teen is lucky, he or she already hits it off well with at least one teacher. But perhaps you've heard these phrases come out of your teen's mouth: "I can't do anything right in this class. My teacher hates me."

It can be hard to sort out how much of the statement is truth, a one-sided perception, or an excuse for not taking responsibility in the class. Where I've landed—after many conversations and the passage of time—is that there's probably a little bit of all three things going on.

If you notice that your teen isn't connecting well with most or *any* teachers, by all means speak up. Talk to the high school counselor or principal. Ask parents with older siblings about memorable teachers. It's critical that your teen build a relationship with an adult at school, someone who's trustworthy, a good listener, and a potential advocate. It doesn't have to be just a teacher. For example, it could be the janitor or person responsible for closing up after drama club, a regular volunteer in a science or art class, or a counselor.

When my husband and I saw that our daughter's grades

were slipping in 10th grade—and we knew she had plenty of ability to succeed—we found out from talking to her that she simply didn't feel connected to school. We asked her counselor to help us identify some teachers who would make an effort to get to know her. A few schedule changes that better connected her to teachers with a reputation for relating well made a wonderful difference. To this day, one of those teachers remains her mentor. He saw her gifts—as student and person—and helped her channel them academically and for her own personal growth.

The truth is some teachers shouldn't be teaching. They don't like being with young people or they need a break. It's important to listen seriously when our kids point out a rocky relationship with a teacher, while at the same time helping them see and accept their role in keeping a relationship strong. Their efforts help build their ability to work well with all kinds of people.

Most of us can remember a special teacher who refused to give up on us, saw past our silly behavior or blank face, reached through our extreme shyness, or called attention to a gift no one had seen before. Ask your teen which teachers stand out for them, and be sure to let those teachers know you appreciate their efforts! My daughter did that once for a special middle school teacher. A year later, I ran into her and she pulled the tattered note out of her purse and told me that note meant so much to her, she kept it with her all the time. Good teachers give it their best, but often have no idea whether what they did made a difference. Take time to tell them.

16

Retirees

By some estimates, 87 million adults now in the United States were born between 1946 and 1964. That bulge in the population is beginning to reach retirement age—many in great health, both physically and financially. With a movement afoot that's reframing this period in an adult's life as "*refirement*" (check out www.refirement.com), many retirees are looking at how to refocus their energies. Some see that new focus as connecting with young people—from volunteering in schools and museums to mentoring at businesses and supporting neighborhoods.

Henk Newenhouse of Lone Rock, Wisconsin, hit upon the idea to attend the local high school varsity soccer games, but was surprised to discover he was the only nonfamily member on the bleachers. Being the only "outside" fan, he got to know all 18 families on the benches and, through them, all 18 members of the team. Invariably, a current or past soccer player changes his oil, checks his groceries, invites him to graduation parties, and lets him know of successful college acceptances. At the last annual banquet for the team, the player who received the highest award honored Henk with these words: "I want to thank Henk for coming to all our games. It meant a lot to me." Says Henk, "I enjoy very much being around enthusiastic young people. I guess I was seeking that out in my old age."

Shelby Andress, a respected community activist, trainer, and consultant on youth issues, marked the end of her 30-year career at Search Institute with a refirement event and focuses some of her energies to giving young people "pre-employment experience." She hires young people she knows to tend her garden when she travels and do light housekeeping chores she needs help with. She kindly points out how they can improve their service and work habits and praises them honestly when they do well.

As the baby boom reaches retirement age, you may:

- Express to older adults your interest in them spending more time with your teen;

- Tell a retiree that your teen has admired him or her or is looking for some work experience—ask if there are some chores that need tending to;

- Consider asking anyone retiring or nearing retirement in your office to spend time with your teen; or

- Visit local centers for seniors or retirees or contact the local chapter of your American Association of Retired Persons or Canadian Association of Retired Persons, which could also put you in touch with interested retirees.

17

Youth Workers

There's an entire group of professionals who have built their careers around connecting with young people. They are often referred to as *youth workers*. Organizations such as the YMCA and YWCA (both of which also serve families), scouting groups, Camp Fire USA or Guides in Canada, 4-H, Girls and Boys clubs, and youth groups at congregations are filled with caring adults who have chosen youth work and building relationships with young people as their profession.

The YMCA of the USA and YMCA of Canada believe so strongly in the power of developmental assets to help young people succeed and to make communities better, that they've joined Search Institute to create an initiative called Abundant Assets. The idea of this collaboration is to make asset-building activities and ideas available to all young people, families, and communities with whom they have contact—and to strengthen their own organizations and programs. Most make their services affordable to you based on your income. So don't let money be a barrier. How do you find a good fit? Try:

- *Rediscovering these organizations*—many have changed since *you* were teen.

  In the United States, Boy Scouts, for example, now has a co-ed affiliate called Venturing BSA, which describes itself as a youth development program for young men and women who are 14 (and have completed grade 8) through 20 years of age. The program is "based on a unique and dynamic relationship between youth, adult leaders, and organizations in their communities."

  In the United States, Camp Fire isn't just for girls anymore. As the first nonsectarian interracial organization for girls in the United States, its newer coed programs are designed to reduce sex-role as well as racial and cultural stereotypes. The 4-H organization, historically an agriculturally based organization for rural youth, has activities for urban teens, too.

- Considering visiting one or two programs with your teen. Meet the program director and see how well he or she relates to your teen.

- Asking at your congregation if there's a youth minister or youth group religious leader.

- Asking about *developmental assets*—youth organizations that know the term will likely emphasize building strong relationships.

18

A Bookkeeper or Tax Preparer

Do you work with someone who prepares taxes, does book-keeping, or is a financial planner? The next time you visit her or him, bring your teen along. The experience may be as much an opportunity to build a relationship as it is to learn about money issues.

Young people don't typically come in contact with people who have expertise in this area. And yet knowing how to handle money is a practical skill they must acquire as they become adults.

Understanding money helps young people feel empowered. And connecting with a good financial person early in life may be the beginning of a rewarding relationship—in more ways than one, if your teen finds he or she likes the professional and the profession.

A teen who is earning any amount of money can begin to think about saving, investing, giving some to a good cause, and keeping some for spending. A financial planner can help your teen figure out what proportions in each area make sense. Teens may be surprised to find out how much they can save over time by starting small early in life.

Of course, you won't want to ask a money expert to start such a connection during tax season. But during the off-season, you may find that your tax preparer or financial accountant would be open to helping a young person become more financially savvy. It's in his or her interest when things slow down to build a trusting relationship with a potential future client.

19

"Adopted" Grandparents

Whether your teen's "real" grandparents live with you, nearby, in another state or province, or across an ocean, it's enriching to have even more older people become "like family" to your teen. Elders often offer a perspective that teens may find calmer than that of busy parents, and perhaps, more accepting.

I remember Mrs. Waggoner, who lived next door when I was 12 and would invite me for tea, cookies, and conversation. My grandparents lived 2,000 miles away, and she was the next best thing to having my beloved grandmother nearby. I still marvel at how her simple gestures made me feel valued and respected and much older than my chronological age.

In Northfield, Minnesota (a small college town 30 miles south of Minneapolis), senior citizen Lewis Appledoorn has invited his young neighbors to help him with woodworking projects. Not surprisingly, he's become known as "Grandpa" to these young people and is an example of a caring older adult who acts in simple ways to connect with youth in his neighborhood.

Even if you think you don't encounter many older people, for one day, try to pay special attention to who crosses your path.

- Are older neighbors providing daycare for their grandchildren or strolling with them at the park? Could they use a little help from your teen?

- Are older people frequenting a local coffee shop that you usually just zip into for a caffeine fix? Might they enjoy a game of cards, chess, or some other board game with you and your teen?

- Are there homebound elders in your neighborhood, block, apartment complex, or down the road who may know about a subject your teen is struggling with in school? Could you ask him or her to tutor your teen?

- Is there an assisted-living complex on your route to work? Could you stop in and see if they need teen volunteers to play music for, read to, or sing with the residents? To walk their dogs? To just visit?

20

Faith-Based Role Models

If your teen is approaching a faith-based rite of passage or other unique event, use it as an opportunity to include a special adult, even if your faith's ritual or the event doesn't require a sponsor, adult advocate, or friend.

Perhaps when your teen was an infant, you named a godparent or chose an adult to play a special role in her or his life, beginning with a baptism, a *Bris* (circumcision and naming ceremony), or other ritual. Unfortunately, such relationships are often limited to a one-time connection. A teen's upcoming confirmation, *Bar* or *Bat Mitzvah,* or other religious ceremony is a good chance to reconnect.

You also don't need to limit asking just one special adult. Consider inviting more than one to participate.

The Schauer family of Lakeville (a suburb of Minneapolis) decided early on in their children's lives that if two godparents were good, four could be even better. "So many people lead busy lives and are spread so thin, we thought this would be a great way to make sure our kids had caring adults in their lives," says mom Julianne Schauer. Each child has two male and two female godparents. The family chose adults who were not couples, and although the family observes a Catholic tradition, not all the godparents are Catholic.

Here are some ideas to think about:

- If you live far way from relatives, consider choosing one or two sponsors locally for each of your kids and one or two from where other family members live.

- Encourage godparents, sponsors, or other special adults to have ongoing conversations about their faith with your teen. They could pick favorite sacred writings or songs to share with each other.

- Invite the special adults to other occasions that may not be faith-based, such as birthdays, school open houses, awards ceremonies, and other special events.

21

Eyewitnesses to Historic Events

School projects for events such as History Day or career-exploration assignments are natural openers for connections with interesting adults.

When my younger son, Erik, saw the movie *Saving Private Ryan,* it sparked a hunger in him for knowledge about World War II. Not long after, he was required in grade 7 to do an assignment for History Day, an educational event in which U.S. middle and high school students display or perform history-related projects on a particular theme. Not surprisingly, he selected D day as his topic.

I knew that the father of a colleague of mine had flown during the invasion of Normandy, and I asked if she thought he might be willing to be a source for Erik. She checked with her father, and he agreed to be interviewed on videotape (even though he'd never detailed his story for his own family).

As a 13-year-old, Erik had a remarkable opportunity to learn about a major historical event and connect with a fascinating, engaging veteran who was willing to tell his story to educate young people. It was a one-time encounter, but

Erik will never forget that amazing afternoon with the veteran, whose personal telling of the event was as dramatic as any movie could portray.

You may be the one who is most likely to know of people who've been involved in historic events (e.g., Civil Rights marches, Woodstock, the 1972 Summit Series in Canada, the fall of the Berlin wall, the opening of diplomatic relations with the People's Republic of China, an immigration wave), so the first contact may be up to you. Consider, too, individuals who may not have been "involved" in a particular event, but have vivid memories of the reactions at the time (e.g., the bombing of Pearl Harbor, the assassinations of Martin Luther King, Jr. or John F. Kennedy).

As a parent, you can help prepare your son or daughter to engage respectfully with these adults. Since Erik was pretty shy about doing his interview, we sat down together to come up with a list of questions and talked about good manners to use when asking personal questions, like thanking him for being willing to talk, speaking clearly, being careful not to interrupt, trying not to worry if he paused to think and there was a little bit of awkward silence, and so forth. Doing a practice "interview" can be a good idea if your teen is a little nervous.

Of course, if your teen and a History Day source really connect, do what you can to keep the relationship going. Maybe your teen could invite him or her to speak at school. Perhaps they could write something together to have published for a local publication or *The History Channel Magazine,* for example, which accepts submissions of interesting personal stories.

Small Business Owners

The people who run or work at the local deli, coffee shop, bookshop, video or hardware store, pharmacy, or gas station, can be important assets to any community—and potentially friends to your teen.

Tom Garrison, a graduate student in broadcasting in Lincoln, Nebraska, grew up in a small town. When his parents had to work late, they'd give him and his sister some money to eat at the local, small-town cafe. His dad knew Brenda, the manager, and the two had conspired (unbeknownst to Tom) to make sure the siblings ate a healthy meal.

After asking about school, Brenda would make funny negotiations with the two youth when they placed their orders: "You can eat whatever you want, but your dad says you have to drink milk instead of soda tonight" or "You can have cheeseburgers and French fries, but first you have to eat a salad or some green beans," Tom says. "This was our parents' way to stay connected with us when they were unavailable, and Brenda always made us feel as if she was making dinner just for us instead of taking orders from customers."

Not all small business owners realize the ability they have to create a friendly, supportive community for young people, even develop a special connection with some, but those who do often find it's good for business. So be sure to introduce your teen to the owners, managers, and employees of local shops and services. And encourage your teen to be respectful and polite when patronizing local businesses to help build rapport and counter negative stereotypes about teens.

Law Enforcement Officers

A teen's strong relationship with even *one* law enforcement officer could save his or her life.

In Norman, Oklahoma, for example, a teen boy found a gun on his way home from school. Not sure what to do, he hid it at home for several days. When he saw a policeman he knew, though, he asked him, "If I tell you something bad, will you promise not to get me in trouble?" The policeman responded that he'd do his best. The boy told him about the gun, and the two sat down together and wrote up a report about where it was found. The gun did not get accidentally fired and hurt anyone—nor did the boy get into trouble.

Why? The officer and the teen had previously built a relationship of trust through a local after-school program that the boy attended and the officer frequented.

Many law enforcement officers see the value of building connections with young people. Here are a few examples:

- In Iowa Falls, Iowa, the chief of police has restored a vintage patrol car and he volunteers to chauffeur local teens in it for prom.*

- In Creston, Iowa, Sgt. Pat Henry organizes softball games between teens and area police, firefighters, and emergency medical technicians as a way for youth and adults to get to know each other.**

- In Minneapolis, when the city's police force faced budget problems and had to stop providing service at the high schools, the Minneapolis Park Police stepped in as liaisons to the schools. Officer Tom Ryan, who has served more than seven years at Southwest High School, resigned from the city's force and joined the park force so that he could maintain his relationship with the school and students.

The easiest place to start is right in your neighborhood. If your teen's school has a law enforcement officer assigned to it, introduce your teen to him or her and encourage them to get acquainted in a positive way. Or invite a law enforcement agent to your block party and strike up a conversation about the rigors of training for such a career or the most heroic thing he or she has had to do. You could also check with your local police or sheriff's department to see what efforts they have under way to build connections with young people.

---

*White, J. "Assetera . . . Ideas That Work, Opinions That Matter, Research That Illuminates," *Assets Magazine,* Autumn 2002, 5.

**Melba, T. "Union County Unites Diverse Sectors," *Assets Magazine,* Autumn 2001, 11.

24

Artists

Creative teens need safe havens to express their quirky sides, to be recognized for their strengths, to be accepted for their unique qualities, and to be supported in their efforts to stretch their talents. If you have such a teen, connecting her or him to caring adults in organizations that promote the arts is one of the greatest gifts you can give to your teen—and to yourself, especially if being "artsy" is not your thing.

The impulse to create, to be unique, to express themselves artistically is powerful in certain young people and an important part of exploring their identity and finding meaning in their lives. It can also be confusing, even off-putting to more conventional adults, who may see such expressiveness as rebellion, arrogance, or outright defiance.

At an urban Midwestern high school, a group of theater students was able to connect with a professional playwright and director at a local theater who invited them to create a production with her about family stories. The youth had to interview family members, then write a piece for a one-night ensemble event. The performance was extraordinary, and the audience was eager to ask students questions about their work. When Stephen Christensen, 17, was asked whether the process had made him feel more connected to his ancestors, he thought for a moment, then said: "Actually, it made me feel most connected to the relative I interviewed."

Some tips on how to connect your teen to an artist:

- *Check what's happening at school.* Talk with English, music, and visual art teachers to find out if the school has sponsored any "artists in residence" programs with local museums, galleries, community theaters, music groups, or arts organizations. Ask your teen if he or she participated in or saw a performance. See what other opportunities the sponsoring organization has to offer.

- *See if your state or province has an agency* that provides grants for the arts. Grantees may have included working with youth as part of their proposal. The agency should be able to give you contact information for such groups.

- *Pick some nearby museums or galleries* for your teen to visit, or go to together. Many museums have free admission for a day once a week or month including hands-on activities or discussions with an artist or curator. Gallery owners can provide a wealth of information about the art world.

- *See whether any of the local radio stations* or theaters have internships or volunteer opportunities for teens.

III

Adults Who Provide Specialized Services

Numerous adults are great at connecting with teens in a variety of informal day-to-day ways. But when your teen needs to connect with tutors, therapists, and physicians, the specialized services these adults can provide can be a real lifesaver—in more ways than one.

Tutors

If your son or daughter is struggling with a subject and needs some extra help, don't hesitate to find a tutor, even if your teen groans at the mention of it. If it's a good fit, the complaining won't last long.

A good tutor will understand his or her subject area and be able to connect right away with your son or daughter on some level. Successful tutors know how to quickly zero in on any insecurities a student is struggling with, then build up the student's confidence in a hurry.

My husband, Randy, is in great demand as a math tutor, both because of the way he helps students grasp the concepts that they struggle with in the classroom and because he becomes a *friend*—an adult who kids know truly wants them to succeed.

He's had many a conversation with students he tutors that has nothing to do with math. But in connecting with them about wrestling, rap, Harry Potter, being grounded, or getting a job, he builds a rapport that ignites in these students a desire to please him with their progress.

How do you find a good tutor? Here are a couple tips:

- *Word of mouth* is sometimes the best; many families have had to call upon a tutor at some point and can give you a recommendation.

- *Ask your child's teachers*—they are so grateful when their students catch up that they're likely to keep track of the tutors who make a difference.

- *Professional tutoring services* are also available and can be found through your phone book.

26

Formal Mentors

Sometimes, the extra help a struggling teen could use from a caring adult friend is not tutoring in a particular school subject, but in managing the everyday challenges of his or her particular world, whatever that may be—perhaps gaining confidence, getting along better with peers or family, or overcoming the loss of a parent. Finding that rudder to help steer your teen in the right direction can be made easier through the services of various formal mentoring programs, many of which have a strong history of success.

So when you want to find a more formal mentor for your teen, how do you locate one?

Rebecca Saito, an independent researcher and consultant in Minnesota in youth development and mentoring, offers these suggestions:

- *Many different kinds* of mentoring programs are available, besides through such organizations as Big Brothers Big Sisters and United Way—in churches, through family-to-family mentoring or e-mail mentoring. Think about what's going to be the best setting for you son or daughter.

- *Ask whether background checks* have been run on potential mentors.

- *Find out whether the program has* ongoing training for mentors, does a careful matching process, follows up with matches after a month or so to see how things are going, and evaluates its efforts.

- *Make sure you're comfortable* with the philosophical approach of the program; for example, if it's faith-based, does it match up with your beliefs? If not, are you comfortable with it anyway?

- *Big Brothers Big Sisters* is the oldest and largest youth mentoring organization in the United States. It works closely with parents and guardians to match every young person with the right "Big" as the volunteer mentors are called. Every volunteer is screened, trained, and supervised. The youth, or "Littles," get one-on-one time and attention, typically two to four times a month. Through simple friendship and unstructured outings, the Bigs cultivate relationships that provide the youth with skills to better manage whatever particular circumstances they're trying to cope with.

- *Another good place* to check is with your local United Way volunteer center. You should be able to find the listing in your local phone book.

27

Therapists

In the same way that most of us seek a physician's help when our child sprains an ankle, needs a few stitches, or catches strep throat, there are times when we may need the help of a professional for our teen's *mental* health. It's really a sign of strength when anyone (parent or child) recognizes a problem and takes the steps needed to solve it.

I realize that as parents we can feel as if we've failed in our duty to protect when our child gets hurt or sick. We feel even worse when our child is hurting emotionally. But wallowing in worry or guilt won't make the hurt go away.

Remember: while we parents are the most important adults in our children's lives, there are many influences besides us—peers, media, social pressures, to name a few. Other trustworthy adults are some of our best parenting resources. So the first step in your child's ability to heal emotional problems may well be reaching out for the best counseling help possible. The connection your teen forms with a caring, responsible therapist will strengthen her or his ability to get through rocky times now *and* later as an adult.

If your child needs professional help for an emotional or mental health dilemma, picking a reputable therapist is essential. When our family needed such services, we looked specifically for a professional who could see the strengths of adolescents, not just what might be perceived as wrong. It's one of the best things we ever did for our family. Here are some tips for finding a good licensed therapist:

- *Ask around.* Word of mouth is sometimes the best way to get a good recommendation. We asked someone who was a youth worker and who knew about developmental assets.

- *Check with your healthcare provider.* Our family physician was very interested in hearing our recommendations for good therapists. She keeps track of these names for other parents. Your physician may also know whom your teen is likely to connect with.

- *Ask your school counselor, nurse, or social worker.* Some have worked in an independent or clinic setting previously, or are familiar with other community specialists. They may also know which ones focus on particular issues.

- *Check your employee benefits.* Many employee assistance programs provide referral services as well as reduced fees for therapy sessions.

Sometimes, it may take meeting a few therapists before finding one who is best able to help your teen.

28

Physicians

Trust is a critical part of building a strong relationship with a physician, and there may come a time when your teen and his or her physician need time alone. Although you're accustomed to being in the room with your baby, toddler, preschooler, and elementary-age child, it may be time to step out when your child reaches the teen years.

That was a hard one for me at first, but my teens' physicians (each child has his or her own) have built trusting bonds with them. My kids know they can ask questions they might not have felt comfortable asking with me in the room. Because I also trusted these physicians, I could let go, knowing that they'd bring me "into the loop" if necessary.

When Tenessa Gemelke, now living in Columbia Heights, Minnesota, was 10 years old, her mother decided it was important for her to have a primary care doctor who could relate well to her as she matured. She found a wonderful pediatrician who put Tenessa at ease, always remembering to ask about the current school play or congratulate her on her successes in speech competitions.

Although this pediatrician didn't ordinarily work with older children, she did keep Tenessa as a patient until high school graduation. "While my teenage body was going through so many tremendous changes, it was a relief to have a physician I trusted," Tenessa remembers.

If you're looking for a new physician for your child as a teenager, here are some points to consider:

- If your son or daughter's high school has an in-school clinic (or nurse), ask the specialists there if they can recommend a physician who is good at building rapport with teens.

- Some physicians choose a specialty called *adolescent medicine,* but the number of doctors trained in this area is small in comparison to those in *primary care medicine,* who see primarily adults.

- In another specialty, *family medicine,* physicians are trained to treat people along the whole lifespan and to pay attention to a person's emotional needs and how stress can affect her or his health.

- Especially if your teen is physically active, you could consider a physician who specializes in *sports medicine,* a subspecialty of both family medicine and internal medicine. Physicians trained in this area are likely to have a good deal of experience with teens and may even coach, share an interest in, or have played the sports your teen likes.

IV

Activities to Try

Numerous activities provide another path for you, your teen, or both of you to seek out adults interested in and eager to help young people. By joining particular groups—through after-school programs, congregations, community facilities—or by organizing or participating in special events—in the neighborhood, with a local college or a seniors' residence, or volunteer effort—your teen will have plenty of opportunities for safe, caring relationships with adult friends to grow.

Talk to a Neighbor

Great neighborhoods for teens are ones where neighbors know each other by name, talk to each other, gather from time to time, pay attention to what's happening with all the kids, and speak up when things go amiss.

Your neighborhood may be teeming with possibilities for your teen. You might even consider creating a caring adult "map" with your son or daughter of your neighborhood or community and note where there are interesting or caring adults. Do you know their names? Have you ever chatted with them while walking your dog or picking up the mail?

Encourage your neighbors to get to know you and your teen. And encourage your teen to get to know them. Let neighbors know you're okay with them enforcing the boundaries that will keep your neighborhood safe, even if it means calling your teen on something. This may come as a surprise, but in a 2002 survey of youth and adults by Search Institute,* young people said that among the most important actions they'd like to see adults take is reporting teens' misbehavior.

After learning about asset building, Witty Shreves, a mother in St. Louis Park (a suburb of Minneapolis) convinced her teens and some other young people in the neighborhood to rake leaves for neighbors who had difficulty doing it for themselves—elderly people, widows, new moms, people with disabilities. Whenever the grateful recipients ask how they can repay the favor, Witty requests that they spend some time with the young people while they are raking. She's noticed that elderly people tend to be afraid of the teens, but the fear vanishes once they become better acquainted. One retired elderly hockey player made an especially strong connection with a 13-year-old, who did odd jobs for him until he left for college.

Strong neighborhoods appear to make it easier to be a parent, as well. A study** of racially and ethnically diverse urban neighborhoods found that parents who had strong support from neighbors were more warm and responsive as parents. Look at your neighborhood with a fresh eye. Connecting your teen with interesting, interested, and caring neighbors will do both of you a world of good.

---

*Scales, P. C., Benson, P. L., & Mannes, M. 2002. *Grading grown-ups 2002: How do American kids and adults relate?* Minneapolis: Search Institute (download at www.search-institute.org).

**Marshall, N. L., Noonan, A. E., McCartney, K., Mark, F., & Keefe, N. 2001. It takes an urban village: Parenting networks of urban families. *Journal of Family Issues,* 22, 163–182; cited in Scales, P. C. 2003. *Other people's kids: Social expectations and American adults' involvement with children and adolescents.* New York: Kluwer Academic/Plenum Publishers, pp. 7–8.

30

Be a Caddy

Is your teen one of the legions of fans of golf superstar Tiger Woods? Never misses a chance to play miniature golf? Maybe he or she would like to be a caddy.

The thought of carrying a grown-up's golf clubs around may not draw your teen's enthusiasm at first mention. But be sure to point out that golf etiquette suggests that adult golfers treat caddies respectfully—as golf learners—and that they engage cordially with their caddies, getting to know them, asking about school, career plans, and such. And working as a caddie is a great way for teens to make some extra money, enjoy the outdoors, and build up muscle—in addition to tagging alongside some interesting adults.

For young people, especially those who like the game, caddying offers access to experienced players who can help them improve their game. Many of these players have sampled golf courses around the world and can share interesting travel stories with your teen, too.

Several young friends of mine have been caddies, always eager for spring to come around so they can get back out on the course to improve their game and make some interesting connections.

One of them, 16-year-old high school student Jim Larson, says,

> *I've been able to meet some of the most successful people in the community, people with some good life experiences. It helps to have good people skills, so you can laugh and joke around with anyone. My first couple times out there, I was scared out of my mind. But after a while, I began to feel much more sure of myself.*

When I asked Jim to talk about which of these people were nice to him, he said, "All of them!" But a few stood out because they always greeted him in the clubhouse, asked how he was doing in hockey, or actually talked about things like dreams.

Of course, not *all* golfers will be especially good at connecting with young people, but over time, your teen is likely to build friendships with at least a few and will have learned quite a bit in the process.

You or your teen can call local courses to find out what the requirements are for caddies and when to apply. If you know people who belong to a club, give them a call and see if they can offer any tips.

Make Some Music

Music is a powerful way for young people and adults to connect, and an enjoyable one. Both have so much to learn from and to teach each other.

Does your teen play a musical instrument or like to sing? Do you?

Once a year, Chris Fisher (a teacher) and Patty Hoolihan (a writer) of Minneapolis and their children Kaitlin and Kelly gather with a group of music-loving adults and youth friends for an evening of jamming together. It's a family tradition they look forward to attending, one that puts the kids in direct—and fun—connection with numerous caring adults. The event has come to be known as a *music salon*.

Invitees bring a food dish—and an instrument—to share, and the evening takes off. The only rule is that each person has to perform at least one piece, but the piece can be done with someone else or several others. It can even be as simple as playing the old piano standby, "Chopsticks."

This common love of music has given Patty the opening to connect with one young musician who she might not otherwise know if he didn't come to the salon. Now when she sees him at school or in the neigborhood, she always asks how he's doing with the trombone.

Consider having your own music potluck. Or experiment with other kinds of musical gatherings to begin your own family tradition and bring other adults into your teens' lives. If no one in the family plays a musical instrument, gather CDs or tapes to play some music for one another.

32

Volunteer Together

One sure way to surround your teen with caring, responsible adults is to put yourselves in their midst—through a volunteer activity. Research* shows that the kinds of adults who are most likely to report being engaged with young people tend to be the kind who do volunteer work at least monthly.

It may seem hard to fit volunteer activity into busy schedules, but keep in mind that more and more high schools are requiring some kind of service project (or hours) as a graduation requirement. Most people who volunteer report that when the fit is right, the activity actually energizes them and makes them feel good.

Sometimes it's as simple as putting your names on a sign-up sheet at your congregation or community center. Other times you and your teen may have to dig a little deeper to find the activity that appeals to you both. Here are some other tips that may help you:

---

*Scales, P. C., Benson, P. L., & Mannes, M., with Tellett-Royce, N. and Griffin-Wiesner, J. 2002. *Grading grown-ups 2002: How do American kids and adults relate? key findings from a national study.* Minneapolis: Search Institute.

- *Set a target date* for picking the activity.

- *Jot down separate lists* of what might appeal to you. Compare lists and see what you have in common. If nothing is similar, talk about why you chose those activities and see if any capture the other's interest.

- *Divide the research.* Lots of newspapers and newsletters run lists for volunteers. If your teen is a little shy, have him or her do some searching on the Internet (be sure to check if your area has a Healthy Communities • Healthy Youth initiative—see www.search-institute.org) or at the library. You could call places such as United Way, Lutheran Social Services, Habitat for Humanity, the Animal Humane Society, or food shelves.

- *Have your son or daughter ask friends* what kinds of volunteer activities they've participated in and would recommend. Do the same with your adult friends or coworkers. Many people do wonderful volunteer work, but never call attention to it or to themselves.

- When you pick an activity, give it a *trial* run. If an agreed-upon amount of time passes and it's not going as either of you had hoped, revisit the choice. It's possible your teen likes the activity more than you do and will continue on her or his own, which would be great. Or it's possible you both need to try something different. Remember that each experience builds new skills and relationships.

Nominate a Local Hero

Young people are keenly aware of who's supporting them, people they admire like a hero.

Sometimes support from such individuals is actually indirect—they may not really know your teen. One way to help develop the relationship more directly is to hold an "event," together with your teen, to honor that individual. Honoring these adults in informal ways can keep them energized, aware that they do make a difference, and connected to the kids who need them—and appreciate them.

When Marilyn Peplau of Wisconsin, one of Search Institute's trainers, goes to a new town to make a presentation about building developmental assets, she takes a walk and conducts a series of informal interviews with local young people. She asks the teens she runs into during her "person-on-the-street" interviews to name people they can count on in their community. Inevitably, she starts to hear a few names repeated—and at least one or two of those folks are usually among the attendees at her training.

Ask your teen to think about a local person he or she

considers such a "hero," someone who cares about kids and acts on that belief. Maybe it's a neighbor, a teacher, the local independent coffee shop owner, school bus driver, coach, councilperson, or park maintenance worker.

By sending a letter or card to that special person, your teen can thank her or him directly for being such a special person in her or his life and other young people's lives. Or extend an invitation to join you and your teen for a special recognition celebration—a visit to the ice cream store, a special dinner out, or a meal in your home, complete with a dish made by your teen. If you want to add that "the-more-the-merrier" quality to the event, ask a couple of other families to participate and nominate their local heroes, too.

That's what Pat Howell-Blackmore did. For two generations in her Paris, Ontario, neighborhood, LeRoy Williamson has been a "guardian angel," always there to lend a hand raking leaves, shoveling snow, or acting as the "glue" to keep neighbors connected with a casual conversation on the front lawn. To the young people in particular, he is a constant, friendly presence willing to sponsor their fundraising efforts for sports or school trips.

Last summer when Pat began to plan a neighborhood surprise birthday party in honor of LeRoy, she was amazed at how young and old were more than happy to volunteer their help. When the big day came, LeRoy was truly surprised and the party was alive with all ages of neighbors who sang his praises.

Participate in an After-School Program

Almost every kind of interest that teens have can be supported in an after-school program where caring adults provide some direction and guidance.

According to one study* conducted by the YMCA of the USA of unsupervised teens, 74% said they wanted structured programs that help them get better grades, get into college, and give them life skills. Some 63% said they wanted programs that helped them build their leadership skills and work closely with different kinds of people.

My three kids each attended an after-school program called Recreation-plus (Rec-plus, for short), and when my oldest was a young teen, he began chafing a bit about being there, feeling a little too old. Not surprisingly, he started to act out. What did Jerry Peterson, the head of the program,

---

*YMCA of the USA. 2001. *After school for America's teens: A national survey of teen attitudes and behaviors in the hours after school.* Chicago: YMCA of the USA.

do? Turned Sean into a volunteer, even providing him with a nametag that announced his new status. It kept Sean actively involved in the program the rest of the year and helped him win an award from the Minneapolis Park Board.

Jerry is a sterling example of the kind of adults in after-school programs who enrich the lives of young people during out-of-school hours. He understands what a young person's individual needs are for growth, and he finds ways to meet those needs. In many ways, Sean's behavior today as a soccer coach for younger teens reminds me of Jerry's best qualities. Clearly, Jerry was an excellent role model.

Especially worth checking out are programs that know about and incorporate developmental assets. Search Institute research shows that strong after-school programs have staff who pay special attention to building family-like relationships with young people, creating a safe and stimulating environment, and offering both innovative and tried-and-true activities.

If you'd like more information about good after-school programs in which your teen can connect with caring adults, check with the administration at your child's school for recommendations, or at your local community center, congregation, the Park and Recreation Department, or United Way.

Join a Congregation

Few institutions today bring together youth, adults, and elders regularly for ongoing activities. Congregations are an exception. They are one of the most convenient places where people of different age groups can gather, whatever the faith. And they provide a wonderful place to talk about and affirm the values we choose to instill in our children.

When Anne Lucasse of Minneapolis became a single parent, she made a conscious choice to join a congregation that clearly cared about involving and honoring young people. She and her two children, one teen and one preteen, began to attend regularly as a way to surround her and them with support and caring adults. After they'd attended for a while, her son, Tim, told his mother that he found the congregation "full of light." When she agreed with him that this congregation did seem to be better lit than their previous church, he corrected her: he was referring to the people.

Research* shows that young people who have a healthy connection to a congregation are less likely to try risky behaviors and more likely to make choices that help them succeed: helping others, serving as leaders, and doing well in school.

No matter how you nurture your own spirituality, consider encouraging your teen to stay in or become connected to a congregation that supports the values you hope to reinforce and whose adult members value youth.

If you think your current church, synagogue, mosque, or other type of congregation has the potential to be a good fit but isn't doing quite as much as you'd like for young people, talk to the leaders and other parents to see what can be done to make it a better place for young people and adults to interact.

If you decide to look for a new congregation, find out:

- Is there a youth director?

- Are any services arranged by or designed for teens?

- Does the congregation offer service-learning activities that bring youth and adults together?

- Is there a confirmation process or rite of passage that links a teen with an adult sponsor or mentor?

- What kinds of leadership opportunities do young people have that give them a voice and allow them to work in partnership with adults?

- Is the congregation stating values that match yours?

---

*Scales, P. C., & Leffert, N. 2004. *Developmental assets: a synthesis of the scientific research on adolescent development,* 2d ed. Minneapolis: Search Institute, p.102–103.

36

Explore a University or College

Is there a university, college, community or junior college, or technical school in your community? Does it offer degrees, training, or programs in education, social work, human or youth development, psychology, nursing, or community health? These departments often involve educating adults about young people and require training that involves *contact* with children and teens—through research efforts, special projects, student teaching, pilot programs, and surveys.

Here's an example: Working with a community initiative in South Bend, Indiana, students at Notre Dame University designed a unique eight-week course for teens and seniors.* They helped middle and high school students to teach older adults how to navigate the Internet. One senior learned how to set up e-mail but was at first disappointed because her inbox remained empty. Her teen partner gave her his address and they exchanged e-mails.

It was a wonderful way to develop a relationship be-

---

*Fisher, D. "New Generation Mentors," *Assets Magazine,* Autumn 2002, 10.

tween a teen and an older adult, especially in the context of youth building an empowerment asset: being a resource to the community. And it was made possible because of a connection to an education program.

How do you connect your child with opportunities?

- Institutions of higher education sometimes advertise for participants in such programs, so watch for announcements in your newspaper or on the radio.

- Call a specific department at the college or university and ask what opportunities they may have.

- Some higher education facilities maintain good contacts with teachers or administrators at local middle or high schools. Your teen's school may be one of them. Ask the principal, a counselor, social worker, psychologist, or nurse if they're in contact with a college or university looking for teen participants.

- Teachers in high schools or middle schools who always seem to have a student teacher in the classroom are likely seen as good mentors for college students. Ask those teachers if they have contacts with programs that might connect your teen with other educators involved in innovative activities.

In addition to connecting your teen with interesting, very likely ambitious young adults, these kinds of programs expose them to what life can be like at college or university and help them think ahead.

37

Open Up Your Book Group

If you join a group of adults regularly to talk books, consider opening the group up once or twice a year to your teens. Hearing other book club members share their observations and stories will help your teen get to know the other adults in an interesting way and may encourage them to start up friendships based on what they find they have in common.

It's a great opportunity to pick a book of interest to both generations, too, or suggest that the group read (or re-read) a book that the teens are assigned in an English class. Centering your conversation on that book will give the teens a special advantage—the benefit of all of your insights when the teen has to talk about the book in class, or vice versa, the benefit of the class's insight when your teen contributes to the book group conversation.

Talking about books with adults also offers teens an excellent opportunity to explore many topics of interest to teens:

• How others get through difficult situations.

- Seeing that many of the feelings they're experiencing are universal ones (so they're really not the odd ducks they often think they are)!

- Understanding what other people experience in situations or environments that are very different from their own.

Before the group begins discussing the selected book, consider doing an icebreaker activity. In one fun opener, called two truths and a lie, you tell three things about yourself, two of which are true and one of which is a fib. The rest of the group tries to figure out which statement is not true. It often leads to some good chuckles and a bit of amazement. You could even adapt the activity, on the basis of the book read and its characters, by telling a truth or lie that parallels something in the book.

Sample Another Culture in a Class

Learn sign language, build and play a drum, make sushi, construct a canoe, try step dancing—community education classes can expose your teen *and* you to interesting, often unfamiliar cultures that may differ from your own—and to knowledgeable adults who are enthusiastic teachers.

Building comfort and familiarity with people of other cultural backgrounds is one of the 40 developmental assets, but it's sometimes hard to figure out how to do this without feeling awkward or out of place. Organizers and teachers of beginner classes *expect* that you'll come in with little or no knowledge, and this can help reduce the worry of trying something totally different than what you're accustomed to doing.

You can find classes that explore a variety of cultural topics through such groups as:

- Art and history museums,

- Extension services offered through state universities,

- Community education programs,

- School districts,

- Parks and community centers, and

- Organizations dedicated to preserving the tradition of specific cultures or ethnicities.

Teens may well catch on faster than many of the adult learners, which can give them a real confidence boost. If your class or teacher is particularly inspiring, your teen may choose to advance his or her skills with additional instruction or one-on-one mentoring with the teacher. At some point, your teen may even develop a kind of expertise—and become a teacher, too, or a teacher's assistant. The benefits of taking a class together can multiply quickly.

Adults who are eager to learn something new may also be open to getting acquainted with a young person. So there's the added benefit of potentially connecting with other adult learners in the class.

39

Check Out America's Promise

In Oklahoma City, teens are interviewing war veterans to capture their stories for a national effort to preserve such personal histories. It is just one city among a growing number of "cities of promise" around the country, where groups of caring adults have organized initiatives to link up with the national nonprofit organization, America's Promise—The Alliance for Youth, to make sure young people have the following resources (promises) in their lives:

1. Ongoing relationships with caring adults—parents, mentors, tutors, or coaches.

2. Safe places with structured activities during non-school hours.

3. A healthy start and future.

4. Marketable skills through effective education.

5. Opportunities to give back through community service.

America's Promise was founded after the Presidents' Summit for America's Future in 1997, where U.S. presidents Bill Clinton, George H. W. Bush, Gerald Ford, Jimmy Carter, and Ronald Reagan represented by Nancy Reagan, in an unprecedented gathering, stood together and challenged the nation to make children and youth a national priority and fulfill the Five Promises.

As of today, hundreds of cities, towns, schools, universities, and neighborhoods have committed themselves to fulfilling the five promises. You can find out if you live in a "community of promise" by:

- Visiting www.americaspromise.org,

- Calling (703) 684-4500, or

- Writing to America's Promise—Alliance for Youth, 909 North Washington Street, Suite 400, Alexandria, Virginia 22314-1556.

Communities of promise, which are committed to building developmental assets, have many service-learning endeavors, fun activities, and opportunities (such as in Oklahoma) to introduce your teen to interesting, caring adults. These activities and opportunities are listed at many of the Web sites, called *promise stations*.

40

Befriend a "Newcomer" Family

Are you seeing newsletters or announcements from your teen's middle or high school translated into several languages? Is the ethnic foods section of your grocery store expanding with new offerings? Your town, city, community, or region may be in the midst of resettling a wave of refugee or immigrant families in search of friendly, helpful people and new opportunities.

You and your teen, perhaps? "Adopting" an immigrant family through your congregation, school, neighborhood group, or civic organization is an excellent way to help others—and to connect your teen to some interesting people.

Immigrants and refugees from conflict-troubled countries and areas, such as Somalia, Sudan, Ethiopia, Central America, Laos, and the Balkans, are coming to North America in search of relief from war, persecution, starvation, and extreme poverty. Mary Pipher, Ph.D., author of *Middle of Everywhere: Helping Refugees Enter the American Community* (Orlando: Harcourt, Inc., 2002), paints a fascinating picture of how such "newcomer" families have survived, what their strengths are, and how poignant their need is for even the most basic kinds of information and friendship.

Their efforts to save their families have been heroic, and yet their stories are largely untold. Many have lost a strong community or village life that supported children and are unable to continue working in their educated profession (e.g., medicine) because of different licensing standards in the United States.

For starters, recommends Pipher, immigrant families need to hear these words: "Hello, you are welcome here." Having involved her own young adult children in efforts to welcome refugee or immigrant families, Pipher says she has learned as much about the United States as about the geography, politics, culture, and history of many other countries. Helping any immigrant family fit into the mainstream of American life and economics, Pipher urges, is critical to the future health of us all.

41

Explore Your Roots

Part of being comfortable with people from a variety of backgrounds is knowing and being comfortable with one's *own* ethnicity or culture. Adolescence is a time of exploring identity, and that includes getting to know the traditions, folklore, language, arts, history, and richness of those who came before us.

Even if we as parents haven't done this exploration, helping our children do it is a way to engage them with interesting adults—and help them feel good about their roots. You can connect your teen to caring adults who know something about your own or your teen's own cultural or ethnic heritage through:

- *Special camps*—In Utica, Mississippi, for example, the Henry S. Jacobs Camp provides a place for young people to explore Judaism's rich cultural heritage in an environment that is intentionally building assets.

- *Language camps* are another way to introduce your teen to their roots (see the Web site accessed March 8,

2004 for a list of language camps for young people in North and Central America: www.swopnet.com/ geo_rodeowriter_2000/lang_camps.html).

- *Relatives*—Diana Yellowhammer, an Ojibwe mother in Crystal, Minnesota, encourages her two children to learn family traditions from older generations of relatives. "My auntie made my daughter an outfit so she can dance at powwows," she says, proudly showing photographs of Joyce in a beautifully stitched costume. Her son, Layton, has also learned to gather wild rice with his grandfather and uncles. She adds: "*I* never even learned to do that!"

    Think about a relative you know, but maybe haven't seen in a while, who has a traditional skill your teen would enjoy learning.

- *Community education classes*—High schools and community centers often offer cooking, craft, and language classes that have a special ethnic or cultural focus.

- *Go to a film festival*—Meet the directors, sponsors, filmmakers, and other festivalgoers who are interested in films from a variety of cultures. Find out if there are opportunities to volunteer on the making of a film.

Take a Leadership Role

Some teens are born leaders, they know it, and they look for ways to be influential. Others have promise as leaders but need a little practice and guidance. Some don't see themselves as leaders at all, though their peers might regard them as such.

If your teen is inclined to lead, is seen as a role model, or has strong or thoughtful opinions, he or she may enjoy exploring those qualities in partnership with adults on a nonprofit, community, or school board or committee.

The possibilities for youth leadership these days have grown far more diverse than being elected president of student council. Growing numbers of adults in organizations that serve communities believe that having young people working "shoulder to shoulder" in leadership positions is key to fulfilling their mission.

In Hampton, Virginia, where a strong asset-building initiative flourishes, teens serve on the city Arts Commission and Parks and Recreation Advisory Board. Two high school students hold paid positions in the Planning Department.

Often, agencies and nonprofits recruit for leadership positions from among the young people who volunteer. Others get the word out informally or advertise through schools, in print, or on radio, cable, the Web, or television. You can check with your local United Way agency, congregation, or neighborhood or community organizations to see what opportunities there are for youth leadership on boards, committees, or particular projects or programs.

To help your teen find the best opportunities and the chance to foster a one-on-one relationship, make sure that young people in the organization:

- Are working collaboratively *with* adults;

- Are handling responsibilities that use their gifts;

- Are focusing their efforts as much on building relationships as on accomplishing tasks;

- Are given plenty of orientation, not just plunked down in the middle of meetings and expected to catch on and instantly contribute;

- Are attending meetings set at convenient times, and are run in a way to make things fun;

- Have the adults check in frequently with them to see how their experience is going; and

- Are not burdened with being *the* lone representative of youth voice.

43

Go to a Meeting Together

Traffic congestion, curfews, unwelcome businesses, an upswing in crime, candidate debates, park improvements, affordable housing, budget challenges—all are issues that can draw a crowd to neighborhood or community meetings. Such meetings also appear to draw the kinds of adults who tend to connect with young people.

In a recent national poll* asking 2,000 American adults questions about how connected they were with young people, Search Institute found that those who participated in community activities, such as volunteering or going to neighborhood meetings, were more likely to be positively engaged with young people.

Have you found yourself wondering about an issue, asking, "Isn't there something I can do to change this situation?" Has your teen? Take a small step—go to a meeting together

---

*Scales, P. C., Benson, P. L., & Mannes, M. 2002. *Grading grown-ups 2002: How do American kids and adults relate?* Minneapolis: Search Institute (download at www.search-institute.org).

to learn more and hear what other concerned people are saying or asking.

Be prepared. Before you go to the meeting, discuss with your teen how sometimes meetings can get heated. Suggest that your teen make a point to observe who is most effective at getting a point across and why.

At the meeting, if you hear someone ask a question or make a comment that makes sense or inspires you, introduce yourself and your teen to that person after the event, and find out if there are any opportunities presented for you and your teen to work to make change. Going to a neighborhood meeting is an excellent—and easy—way to expose your teen to how the civic world works and to boost the chances he or she will connect with caring adults who are interested in hearing what teens have to say.

Organize a Block Party

If you're new to a neighborhood or haven't really gotten to know some new neighbors well yet, volunteer to organize or help a committee that is planning a block party as a way to introduce your teen and yourself to the people who live near you. The people who take the task on from year to year would most likely welcome fresh help. And if no one has organized one for a while (or ever), you'll be the hero for taking it on.

Block parties are also an excellent opportunity to introduce neighbors to the concept of developmental assets and the important role they play in creating a supportive network of adults for children as well as teens.

One fun activity that illustrates the importance of developmental assets—and gets youth and adults connecting—comes from a very active asset-building coalition in Alaska. All you'll need is a big ball of multicolored yarn and balloons.

- Have adults form a circle and pass the yarn across the circle 19 times so that they start to form a "web" of yarn. (Each time the yarn is passed, the person holds on to a part of it.) Mention that each strand of the yarn represents an asset—a "nutrient" of success for young people.

- Have each young person blow up a balloon to represent herself or himself. Have the young people toss their balloons onto the "web."

- You'll notice that there are gaps through which the balloons can fall. Mention that unless we close those gaps by building more assets, young people don't have the safety net they need to protect them.

- Next, pass the yarn across the circle of adults 21 more times, until you have a web with 40 strands.

- Have the youth toss their balloons onto the web and observe that there are no more gaps. Cheer their success.

Notice as a group that the web also looks like a "dream catcher"—a handcrafted symbol that many American Indian cultures use with children to protect them from bad dreams and catch the good ones. Mention that when we all build assets together, we keep our young people safe and make it possible for them to reach for their dreams.

45

Put On a "Seniors" Prom

Do you have a knack for planning entertaining get-togethers or organizing events? Consider working with your teen and his or her high school or congregation to put on a dance that brings together senior citizens and senior high school students. Student council, parent-teacher associations, and youth groups are good places to start the ball rolling.

The idea has been a big hit in Los Alamos, New Mexico, where teens and elders have two-stepped, swung, and whirled around the dance floor during Seniors Prom for an evening of intergenerational merriment.* In the Abingtons, a group of eight municipalities near Scranton, Pennsylvania, high school students organized a similar event at a local retirement home.

In the beginning, it can be a little awkward, according to Lil Ortega, who was the 1998 high school senior class sponsor in Los Alamos. "But eventually the kids ask the se-

---

*"Swinging across a generation 'gap,'" *Assets Magazine,* Summer 1998, 4.

nior citizens to dance. And before long, the older folks ask the young folks."

Music has been provided by the Los Alamos Jazz Band, and the older generation has shown the younger ones how to two-step and do the Charleston. "The older people don't have the inhibitions the young ones do," according to Ortega. "Everyone ends up laughing and having a fun time." Some teens have even been inspired to take ballroom dancing lessons at the senior citizens center, making it possible for them to build friendships.

46

Start a Silent Mentoring Effort

For a new spin on the old school staff appreciation theme—and to create a surprising bond between students and adults in your teen's school—consider launching a silent mentoring effort.

In Mason City, Iowa, students in middle and high schools put up the names of all staff members, and each young person put a sticker by the names of the adults he or she knew.[*] Then everyone picked a name of a teacher or staff member they didn't know well to silent mentor during the year. Students made small gifts to give to their secret pals once a month, and identities were revealed at a year-end party.

"I don't think kids realized the impact they were having," says Mary Schissel, coordinator of a local asset-building initiative. But 17-year-old Jessica Higgins from Newman Catholic High School certainly did when her pal, teacher Carolyn Hill, made this observation: "I was going through a very

---

[*]Melby, T. "Getting Kids in the Schoolhouse Door," *Assets Magazine,* Spring 2002, 10–11.

rough time in my life while Jessica was leaving Hershey's Kisses with hearts on my desk. What she did was just like a ray of sunshine. It meant a lot to me."

If you're interested in trying this idea out, you can ask to meet with your teen's middle or high school student council or parent-teacher association and offer to help coordinate. Another way to show appreciation is providing a stack of blank notes outside of a teacher's door where students can leave anonymous notes of gratitude. Mention how this idea is a great way to build a more caring school atmosphere, as well as create a new relationship with an adult at your school.

RESOURCES

-or-

What to remember when nagging worries waylay your good intentions to connect your teen to caring adults

I don't have time to find other adults to be in my kid's life.

Time may be short, but think about how important it is to connect your teen with other adults and where this goal fits in with your priorities. Remember that through relationships with caring adults, your teen can build the developmental assets necessary to help her or him make strong, healthy choices.

Consider the people that you do spend your time with—coworkers, for example, or extended family members. Ask them if they'd spend a little time with your son or daughter, especially if they share an interest. A few minutes during coffee breaks or on the phone may be all it takes to connect your teen with someone who may become very important in both of your lives.

2

What if my teen resists another adult's attention and doesn't want any more adults in his or her life?

A young person can never have too many supportive, trustworthy adults in his or her life. If the problem is that your teen is shy, take a look at the frequently stated worry about shy teens (3).

If your teen just seems to resist attempts by adults to connect, it may take some time—and your extra help. So keep trying. The resistance perhaps indicates an even greater reason to make the effort and ensure that caring, responsible adults are involved in your teen's life. Try to talk with your teen and find out why he or she is so resistant to someone's support.

Some teens need to see that adults aren't going to give up on them, no matter how much they seem to put up obstacles. Think back on someone who refused to give up on you and how memorable that was.

You might also try some activities that you and your teen could do *together* with other caring adults. The most important thing is to keep trying.

3

My teen is just too shy.

Even painfully shy youth need as many caring adults in their lives as they can get. Make sure teachers understand that your teen is shy, not necessarily disinterested. Let neighbors (or *any* trustworthy adult your teen comes into contact with) know the same; some people mistake shyness for arrogance or defiance and add insult to injury by acting in less than kind ways.

Most people who realize shyness is the problem are more likely to be understanding and keep trying little ways to make a connection. Encourage them not to give up. Sometimes, a shy *adult* is a good match for a shy teen.

Remember also how important it is for your teen to learn skills to move through the shyness—and that a caring, accepting adult may be more likely to provide that support than peers. If the shyness is of an extreme nature, finding a sensitive therapist or counselor might be worth a try.

4

What tips can I give an adult for starting up a conversation (or even making small talk) with my teen?

Weird weather, new fads, sporting events, current movies, popular songs, favorite television shows, funny commercials, new software, popular games, controversial comedians, favorite books, and news events all make good topics for starting a conversation. Suggest they try to ask open-ended questions, rather than ones that will get only a yes or no answer. And if questions don't work, how about trying an observation. Sometimes with young people, my husband (a tutor) will make such outlandish observations that no one can resist responding.

My teen balks at any idea I suggest.

Make it someone else's idea! As a parent, you've probably experienced many instances when your teen's reaction to an idea you've suggested was a total lack of expression, but the same recommendation from an admired peer, older sibling, teacher, or someone else got quite a different response—one of interest or curiosity and action.

If you think your teen won't react positively to your talking to him or her about getting more adults involved in his or her life, get someone else on board to help you, someone you know your teen will respond to with some consideration.

6

I can't imagine anyone wanting to spend time with my surly, mouthy teen.

Neither could I, but lots of other people did. Try not to assume that your issues or conflicts with your teen will be the same for others. That old adage about some people seeing a glass half full and others seeing it half empty readily applies to raising teens. What sounds like an attitude to you may come across as a gutsy quality to another adult. What looks to you like a scowl may appear like the makings of a fine actor to someone else. If you hear people marvel at what seem like antics or defiance to you, you may well be hearing the signals of someone who'll connect with your teen. So don't hesitate to share what's going on in your life with teens and ask for help.

7

What if I ask a friend and get turned down? I worry that *my* relationship with that adult will suffer.

Remember that you are doing a wonderful thing for your teen by connecting them to good adults, and by simply asking, you're making the first step toward changing expectations for the better about adults connecting with young people. Not everyone's going to be ready to accept, and that's okay. Some changes take time. Try not to take it personally if your friend turns you down—and remember to be reassuring to your friend, too. Some day, he or she may see others connecting with teens and understand the value at that point. You really want people who want to be with your teen, so it's better if your friend says no now, rather than gets into something he or she won't enjoy.

What if the adult teaches my teens things I disagree with?

It's certainly good to discuss your concerns with the adult as well as with your teen. Remember, too, that your teen is learning to think more independently during these years, and that is something you should encourage. As you well know, your teen isn't always going to agree with you. And as parents, we can't completely shield our children from what we dislike, but we can model good judgment and help them make good decisions (sometimes through the mistakes they make). Never underestimate how much influence you and your values exert on your children. You really are their first and best teacher, and what they learn from you is the yardstick with which they measure what they learn from others.

What if the relationship goes badly or the adult rejects my teen?

Conflicts and misunderstandings in any relationship are inevitable. Perhaps your teen hasn't been rejected, but there's been a disagreement that can be resolved with a little extra effort. It could be a great opportunity to help your teen learn how to patch things up with a friend. On the other hand, not all friendships last, with adults or young people. It's possible you may have to help your teen understand this and move on.

What if the adult doesn't carry through?

If it's clear the adult just isn't responsible enough to follow through on commitments, it's wise not to encourage a connection with him or her.

What if my child forms a stronger bond with another adult than with me?

The bond you have with your child as her or his parent will always be a powerful one, even if it feels incredibly rocky at times. The connections your teen makes with other, caring, trustworthy adults, especially during turbulent times with you, will ultimately shore up her or his ability to smooth any rough patches with you. I've seen this happen in my own family. I bet you're more likely to feel relief that your teen has other caring adults rather than regret.

What Are the Developmental Assets?

The developmental assets are a set of positive qualities, skills, experiences, and opportunities that are critical to develop during adolescent years, helping youth to become caring, reliable adults. Spread across eight broad areas of human development, these assets paint a picture of the positive things all young people need to grow up healthy and responsible. The first four asset categories focus on external structures, relationships, and activities that create a positive environment for young people.

 Support—Young people need to be surrounded by people who love, care for, appreciate, and accept them. They need to know that they belong and that they are not alone.

 Empowerment—Young people need to feel valued and valuable. This happens when youth feel safe, when they believe that they are liked and respected, and when they contribute to their families and communities.

 Boundaries and Expectations—Young people need the positive influence of peers and adults who encourage them to be and do their best. Youth also need clear rules about appropriate behavior and consistent, reasonable consequences for breaking those rules.

 Constructive Use of Time—Young people need opportunities—outside of school—to learn and develop new skills and interests and to spend enjoyable time interacting with other youth and adults.

The next four categories reflect internal values, skills, and beliefs that young people also need to develop to fully engage with and function in the world around them:

 Commitment to Learning—Young people need a variety of learning experiences, including the desire for academic success, a sense of the lasting importance of learning, and a belief in their own abilities.

 Positive Values—Young people need to develop strong guiding values or principles, including caring about others, having high standards for personal character, and believing in protecting their own well-being.

 Social Competencies—Young people need to develop the skills to interact effectively with others, to make difficult decisions and choices, and to cope with new situations.

Positive Identity—Young people need to believe in their own self-worth, to feel that they have control over the things that happen to them, and to have a sense of purpose in life as well as a positive view of the future.

Search Institute has identified the following "building blocks" of healthy development that help young people grow up healthy, caring, and responsible.

EXTERNAL ASSETS

SUPPORT

1. **Family support**—Family life provides high levels of love and support.

2. **Positive family communication**—Young person and her or his parent(s) communicate positively, and young person is willing to seek advice and counsel from parents.

3. **Other adult relationships**—Young person receives support from three or more nonparent adults.

4. **Caring neighborhood**—Young person experiences caring neighbors.

5. **Caring school climate**—School provides a caring, encouraging environment.

6. **Parent involvement in schooling**—Parent(s) are actively involved in helping young person succeed in school.

EMPOWERMENT

7. **Community values youth**—Young person perceives that adults in the community value youth.

8. **Youth as resources**—Young people are given useful roles in the community.

9. **Service to others**—Young person serves in the community one hour or more per week.

10. **Safety**—Young person feels safe at home, at school, and in the neighborhood.

EXTERNAL ASSETS

BOUNDARIES AND EXPECTATIONS

11. **Family boundaries**—Family has clear rules and consequences and monitors the young person's whereabouts.

12. **School boundaries**—School provides clear rules and consequences.

13. **Neighborhood boundaries**—Neighbors take responsibility for monitoring young people's behavior.

14. **Adult role models**—Parent(s) and other adults model positive, responsible behavior.

15. **Positive peer influence**—Young person's best friends model responsible behavior.

16. **High expectations**—Both parent(s) and teachers encourage the young person to do well.

CONSTRUCTIVE USE OF TIME

17. **Creative activities**—Young person spends three or more hours per week in lessons or practice in music, theater, or other arts.

18. **Youth programs**—Young person spends three or more hours per week in sports, clubs, or organizations at school and/or in the community.

19. **Religious community**—Young person spends one or more hours per week in activities in a religious institution.

20. **Time at home**—Young person is out with friends "with nothing special to do" two or fewer nights per week.

INTERNAL ASSETS

COMMITMENT TO LEARNING

21. **Achievement motivation**—Young person is motivated to do well in school.

22. **School engagement**—Young person is actively engaged in learning.

23. **Homework**—Young person reports doing at least one hour of homework every school day.

24. **Bonding to school**—Young person cares about her or his school.

25. **Reading for pleasure**—Young person reads for pleasure three or more hours per week.

POSITIVE VALUES

26. **Caring**—Young person places high value on helping other people.

27. **Equality and social justice**—Young person places high value on promoting equality and reducing hunger and poverty.

28. **Integrity**—Young person acts on convictions and stands up for her or his beliefs.

29. **Honesty**—Young person "tells the truth even when it is not easy."

30. **Responsibility**—Young person accepts and takes personal responsibility.

31. **Restraint**—Young person believes it is important not to be sexually active or to use alcohol or other drugs.

INTERNAL ASSETS

SOCIAL COMPETENCIES

32. Planning and decision making—Young person knows how to plan ahead and make choices.

33. Interpersonal competence—Young person has empathy, sensitivity, and friendship skills.

34. Cultural competence—Young person has knowledge of and comfort with people of different cultural/racial/ethnic backgrounds.

35. Resistance skills—Young person can resist negative peer pressure and dangerous situations.

36. Peaceful conflict resolution—Young person seeks to resolve conflict nonviolently.

POSITIVE IDENTITY

37. Personal power—Young person feels he or she has control over "things that happen to me."

38. Self-esteem—Young person reports having a high self-esteem.

39. Sense of purpose—Young person reports that "my life has a purpose."

40. Positive view of personal future—Young person is optimistic about her or his personal future.

La investigación realizada por el Instituto Search ha identificado los siguientes elementos fundamentales del desarrollo como instrumentos para ayudar a los jóvenes a crecer sanos, interesados en el bienestar común y a ser responsables.

Elementos Fundamentales Externos

APOYO

1. **Apoyo familiar**—La vida familiar brinda altos niveles de amor y apoyo.

2. **Comunicación familiar positiva**—El (La) joven y sus padres se comunican positivamente. Los jóvenes están dispuestos a buscar consejo y consuelo en sus padres.

3. **Otras relaciones con adultos**—Además de sus padres, los jóvenes reciben apoyo de tres o más personas adultas que no son sus parientes.

4. **Una comunidad comprometida**—El (La) joven experimenta el interés de sus vecinos por su bienestar.

5. **Un plantel educativo que se interesa por el (la) joven**—La escuela proporciona un ambiente que anima y se preocupa por la juventud.

6. **La participación de los padres en las actividades escolares**—Los padres participan activamente ayudando a los jóvenes a tener éxito en la escuela.

FORTALECIMIENTO

7. **La comunidad valora a la juventud**—El (La) joven percibe que los adultos en la comunidad valoran a la juventud.

8. **La juventud como un recurso**—Se le brinda a los jóvenes la oportunidad de tomar un papel útil en la comunidad.

9. **Servicio a los demás**—La gente joven participa brindando servicios a su comunidad una hora o más a la semana.

10. **Seguridad**—Los jóvenes se sienten seguros en casa, en la escuela y en el vecindario.

ELEMENTOS FUNDAMENTALES EXTERNOS

LÍMITES Y EXPECTATIVAS

11. Límites familiares—La familia tiene reglas y consecuencias bien claras, además vigila las actividades de los jóvenes.

12. Límites escolares—En la escuela proporciona reglas y consecuencias bien claras.

13. Límites vecinales—Los vecinos asumen la responsabilidad de vigilar el comportamiento de los jóvenes.

14. El comportamiento de los adultos como ejemplo—Los padres y otros adultos tienen un comportamiento positivo y responsable.

15. Compañeros como influencia positiva—Los mejores amigos del (la) joven son un buen ejemplo de comportamiento responsable.

16. Altas expectativas—Ambos padres y maestros motivan a los jóvenes para que tengan éxito.

USO CONSTRUCTIVO DEL TIEMPO

17. Actividades creativas—Los jóvenes pasan tres horas o más a la semana en lecciones de música, teatro u otras artes.

18. Programas juveniles—Los jóvenes pasan tres horas o más a la semana practicando algún deporte, o en organizaciones en la escuela o de la comunidad.

19. Comunidad religiosa—Los jóvenes pasan una hora o más a la semana en actividades organizadas por alguna institución religiosa.

20. Tiempo en casa—Los jóvenes conviven con sus amigos "sin nada especial que hacer" dos o pocas noches por semana.

ELEMENTOS FUNDAMENTALES INTERNOS

COMPROMISO CON EL APRENDIZAJE

21. Motivación por sus logros—El (La) joven es motivado(a) para que salga bien en la escuela.

22. Compromiso con la escuela—El (La) joven participa activamente con el aprendizaje.

23. Tarea—El (La) joven debe hacer su tarea escolar por lo menos durante una hora cada día de clases.

24. Preocuparse por la escuela—Al (A la) joven debe importarle su escuela.

25. Leer por placer—El (La) joven lee por placer tres horas o más por semana.

VALORES POSITIVOS

26. Preocuparse por los demás—El (La) joven valora ayudar a los demás.

27. Igualdad y justicia social—Para el (la) joven tiene mucho valor el promover la igualdad y reducir el hambre y la pobreza.

28. Integridad—El (La) joven actúa con convicción y defiende sus creencias.

29. Honestidad—El (La) joven "dice la verdad aún cuando esto no sea fácil".

30. Responsabilidad—El (La) joven acepta y toma responsabilidad por su persona.

31. Abstinencia—El (La) joven cree que es importante no estar activo(a) sexualmente, ni usar alcohol u otras drogas.

ELEMENTOS FUNDAMENTALES INTERNOS

CAPACIDAD SOCIAL

32. **Planeación y toma de decisiones**—El (La) joven sabe cómo planear y hacer elecciones.

33. **Capacidad interpersonal**—El (La) joven es sympático, sensible y hábil para hacer amistades.

34. **Capacidad cultural**—El (La) joven tiene conocimiento de y sabe convivir con gente de diferente marco cultural, racial o étnico.

35. **Habilidad de resistencia**—El (La) joven puede resistir la presión negativa de los compañeros así como las situaciones peligrosas.

36. **Solución pacífica de conflictos**—El (La) joven busca resolver los conflictos sin violencia.

IDENTIDAD POSITIVA

37. **Poder personal**—El (La) joven siente que él o ella tiene el control de "las cosas que le suceden".

38. **Auto-estima**—El (La) joven afirma tener una alta auto-estima.

39. **Sentido de propósito**—El (La) joven afirma que "mi vida tiene un propósito".

40. **Visión positiva del futuro personal**—El (La) joven es optimista sobre su futuro mismo.

Le Search Institute a défini "les pierres angulaires" suivantes qui aident les jeunes à devenir des personnes saines, bienveillantes et responsables.

ACQUIS EXTERNES

SOUTIEN

1. **Soutien familial**—La vie familiale est caractérisée par un degré élevé d'amour et de soutien.

2. **Communication familiale positive**—Le jeune et ses parents communiquent positivement, et le jeune est disposé à leur demander conseil.

3. **Relations avec d'autres adultes**—Le jeune bénéficie de l'appui d'au moins trois adultes autres que ses parents.

4. **Voisinage bienveillant**—Le jeune a des voisins bienveillants.

5. **Milieu scolaire bienveillant**—L'école fournit au jeune un milieu bienveillant et encourageant.

6. **Engagement des parents dans les activités scolaires**—Les parents aident activement le jeune à réussir à l'école.

PRISE EN CHARGE

7. **Valorisation des jeunes par la communauté**—Le jeune perçoit que les adultes dans la communauté accordent de l'importance aux jeunes.

8. **Rôle des jeunes en tant que ressources**—Le jeune se voit confier des rôles utiles dans la communauté.

9. **Service à son prochain**—Le jeune consacre à sa communauté au moins une heure par semaine.

10. **Sécurité**—Le jeune se sent en sécurité à la maison, à l'école et dans le quartier.

Acquis Externes

Limites et attentes

11. **Limites dans la famille**—La famille a des règlements clairs accompagnés de conséquences, et elle surveille les comportements du jeune.

12. **Limite à l'école**—L'école a des règlements clairs accompagnés de conséquences.

13. **Limites dans le quartier**—Les voisins assument la responsabilité de surveiller les comportements du jeune.

14. **Adultes servant de modèles**—Les parents et d'autres adultes dans l'entourage du jeune affichent un comportement positif et responsable.

15. **Influence positive des pairs**—Les meilleurs amis du jeune affichent un comportement responsable.

16. **Attentes élevées**—Les parents et les professeurs du jeune l'encouragent à réussir.

Utilisation constructive du temps

17. **Activités créatives**—Le jeune consacre au moins trois heures par semaine à suivre des cours de musique, de théâtre ou autres, et à mettre ses nouvelles connaissances en pratique.

18. **Programmes jeunesse**—Le jeune consacre au moins trois heures par semaine à des activités sportives, des clubs ou des associations à l'école et/ou dans la communauté.

19. **Communauté religieuse**—Le jeune consacre au moins trois heures par semaine à des activités dans une institution religieuse.

20. **Temps à la maison**—Le jeune sort avec des amis sans but particulier deux ou trois soirs par semaine.

ACQUIS INTERNES

ENGAGEMENT ENVERS L'APPRENTISSAGE

21. Encouragement à la réussite—Le jeune est encouragé à réussir à l'école.

22. Engagement à l'école—Le jeune s'engage activement à apprendre.

23. Devoirs—Le jeune consacre au moins une heure par jour à ses devoirs.

24. Appartenance à l'école—Le jeune se préoccupe de son école.

25. Plaisir de lire—Le jeune lit pour son plaisir au moins trois heures par semaine.

VALEURS POSITIVES

26. Bienveillance—Le jeune estime qu'il est très important d'aider les autres.

27. Égalité et justice sociale—Le jeune accorde beaucoup d'attention à la promotion de l'égalité, et à la réduction de la faim et de la pauvreté.

28. Intégrité—Le jeune agit selon ses convictions et défend ses croyances.

29. Honnêteté—Le jeune "dit la vérité même si ce n'est pas facile".

30. Responsabilité—Le jeune accepte et assume ses propres responsabilités.

31. Abstinence—Le jeune croit qu'il est important d'éviter d'être sexuellement actif et de consommer de l'alcool ou d'autres drogues.

ACQUIS INTERNES

COMPÉTENCES SOCIALES

32. Planification et prise de décisions—Le jeune sait comment planifier à l'avance et faire des choix.

33. Aptitudes interpersonnelles—Le jeune fait preuve d'empathie et de sensibilité, et noue des amitiés.

34. Aptitudes culturelles—Le jeune connaît des personnes d'autres cultures, races et ethnies, et se sent à l'aise avec elles.

35. Résistance—Le jeune est capable de résister à des pressions négatives exercées par ses pairs et à des situations dangereuses.

36. Résolution pacifique de conflits—Le jeune tente de résoudre les conflits sans recourir à la violence.

IDENTITÉ POSITIVE

37. Pouvoir personnel—Le jeune sent qu'il a le contrôle sur les choses qui lui arrivent.

38. Estime de soi—Le jeune affirme avoir un degré élevé d'estime de soi.

39. Sentiment d'utilité—Le jeune croit que sa vie a un sens.

40. Vision positive de l'avenir—Le jeune est optimiste quant à son avenir personnel.

ADDITIONAL SEARCH INSTITUTE RESOURCES

To learn more about the developmental assets, take a look at these resources from Search Institute through our online catalog at www.search-institute.org.

For Parents (and Other Adults)

Tag, You're It! 50 Easy Ways to Connect with Young People by Kathleen Kimball-Baker. This motivating book offers commonsense ideas to connect and build assets with young people. Youth workers, parents, educators, business people, congregation leaders, and anyone who cares about youth will love this book. The *Tag, You're It!* **card deck** and the *Tag, You're It!* **posters** are also specially designed to spark conversations between youth and adults.

"Ask Me Where I'm Going" and Other Revealing Messages from Today's Teens. What teens want to tell the adults in their lives, they tell you here in this gift book in their own evocative words. Their inspirational words will help you to think about ways you can connect with teens to give them what they want—the same things that research shows they need for success.

Parenting at the Speed of Teens: Positive Tips on Everyday Issues. Foreword by Peter L. Benson, PhD. Packed with real dilemmas parents and caregivers face daily with teens, this book helps parents reframe a situation from a positive approach, answers questions in an upbeat, constructive way, and offers hope through practical ideas.

Ideas for Parents. This collection of 52 newsletters introduces the developmental assets and categories to parents each week for a full calendar year. Weekly features include suggestions for how parents can talk with kids and quick practical tips.

Hey Coach! Positive Differences You Can Make for Young People in Sports by Neal Starkman. This resource provides many situations coaches may encounter while working with young people. Through the developmental assets framework, coaches learn how to handle these situations positively to increase participants' enjoyment and personal growth.

In Good Company: Tools to Help Youth and Adults Talk by Franklin W. Nelson. This hands-on workbook includes 8 sets of tear-out sheets with introductory and get-acquainted activities perfect for adults and youth in one-on-one mentoring relationships.

Creating Intergenerational Community: 75 Ideas for Building Relationships between Youth and Adults by Jolene L. Roehlkepartain. Filled with numerous ideas that individual adults, groups of adults, individual youth, and groups of youth can initiate to build bridges across generations.

Taking Asset Building Personally: Planning Guide and Personal Action Workbook. With the planning and discussion guide plus six copies of the Action and Reflection workbook, you'll have everything you need to work in a small parents' group or book club.

Working Shoulder to Shoulder: Stories and Strategies of Youth-Adult Partnerships That Succeed by Deborah Fisher. Adults and youth describe barriers encountered, lessons learned, and shared success. Offers a good combination of philosophy and practical advice for starting and strengthening youth-adult partnerships.

More Than Just a Place to Go: How Developmental Assets Can Strengthen Your Youth Program. Based on three different out-of-school programs this video shows how to intentionally create a developmentally rich environment, staff, and program for young people. The book by the same name offers a more indepth approach.

The Asset Approach (Spanish version available). Informative and concise, this 8-page handout introduces adults to the power of using the 40 developmental assets in daily interactions with young people.

For Teens

Take It to the Next Level: Making Your Life What You Want It to Be by Kathryn (Kay) L. Hong. This booklet helps young people focus on their successes, explore what they really want and how to get it, and celebrate their efforts and accomplishments. Filled with activities and journal topics, it offers a chance for more self-exploration and action than the introductory companion booklet *Me@My Best: Ideas for Staying True to Yourself—Every Day.*

An Asset Builder's Guide to Youth and Money by Jolene L. Roehlke-partain. This practical guide takes a positive approach to empowering young people to build competency in financial areas such as earning, spending, investing, saving, and giving.

Step-by-Step! A Young Person's Guide to Positive Community Change by The Mosaic Youth Center Board members and Jennifer Griffin-Wiesner. Young people provide the ideas and tools for other young people to make change in their community, including how to involve adults to help, and share the tips and trials of their work to get a new community center built in their own neighborhood.

What Teens Need to Succeed: Proven, Practical Ways to Shape Your Own Future by Peter L. Benson, Judy Galbraith, and Pamela Espeland. This engaging book walks teens through the 40 developmental assets providing the power to look at their own lives, celebrate the good parts, identify problem areas, and shape their own success.

ABOUT THE AUTHOR

Kathleen Kimball-Baker is director of Publishing and executive director of Enterprise Services at Search Institute. She has spent 27 years in news reporting, feature writing and editing, and magazine and book publishing in newspapers, healthcare, university, corporate, and nonprofit settings. She and her husband, Randy, live in Minneapolis, Minnesota, where they have found the teen years of their three children, Sean, Laura, and Erik—and their many friends—thoroughly rewarding, often challenging, and full of opportunities for learning and fun. She is also the author of *Tag, You're It! 50 Easy Ways to Connect with Young People,* a book that helps all kinds of adults discover how important, easy, and rewarding it is to build relationships with teens.

ABOUT SEARCH INSTITUTE

Search Institute is an independent, nonprofit, nonsectarian research and education organization whose mission is to provide leadership, knowledge, and resources to promote healthy children, youth, and communities. The institute collaborates with others to promote long-term organizational and cultural change that supports its mission. For a free information packet, call 800-888-7828 or visit our Web site at www.search-institute.org.